Does She Think of Me

A Birth Mother's Journey to Forgiveness

CATHY WILLIAMS-THRUN

Does She Think of Me
Copyright © 2020 by Cathy Williams-Thrun

All rights reserved. No part of this publication may be reproduced, distributed, or transmitted in any form or by any means, including photocopying, recording, or other electronic or mechanical methods, without the prior written permission of the author, except in the case of brief quotations embodied in critical reviews and certain other non-commercial uses permitted by copyright law.

Tellwell Talent
www.tellwell.ca

ISBN
978-0-2288-2250-9 (Hardcover)
978-0-2288-2249-3 (Paperback)
978-0-2288-2251-6 (eBook)

Dedication

My journey to forgiveness ended with the one person brave enough to trust the stranger who bore her, patient enough to let me explain, understanding enough to accept what was and strong enough to give me the only blessing my soul longed for, forgiveness.

To my first born

Kelly

Preface

Writing anything to share with the world, let alone a memoir, was the furthest thing from my mind. Searching for one unique gift is where it all began. Emails stored for over twenty years on six floppy disks was my inspiration. The twentieth anniversary of mine and Kelly's reunion was May 20, 2019. How awesome would it be to compile those emails into a published book for her?

I hadn't looked at the emails since the reunion May 20, 1999, so my first challenge was to get them off the floppy disks because computers no longer use them. I'm really dating myself now! I'm sure you've heard the phrase, "There's an app for that," well there's a device for just about everything, even transferring information from floppy disks to external hard drives.

With the emails safely uploaded to my computer I sat back to read and organize them. I wasn't prepared for the tidal wave of emotions that washed over me. I was instantly transported back to 1999 when I, a birth mother, and Kelly, an adoptee, poured our hearts out in an effort to understand the Why, and to seek forgiveness and acceptance.

This gift had to be perfect, so I set out to find an editor to help me create a book—just one book, that's all. My internet search connected me with Marnie Woodrow, a Canadian writer and editor. I sent her everything I had, literally a scrambled mess! Upon reading the emails she suggested I write a story and incorporate *a couple of the emails,* not all of them. I wasn't overly keen on the idea of writing a memoir but took her advice. After all, if I didn't like the outcome I could go back to my original plan. With each feedback session Marnie encouraged me to publish and, well…here I am.

Marnie, I am so eternally grateful that our paths crossed. Working with you on this project has taken me in a direction I never imagined. I loved the experience and the process. Step by step, chapter by chapter, you guided me to this moment. I had a story to tell and you were instrumental in helping me express it to the best of my ability. You held me to task. Some days the words from my past were so painful to write that I found myself standing in the bathroom sobbing. I would splash cold water on my face, take a deep breath and get back to my desk because I had a deadline to meet. What I love about you is that you treated me like an author. You made me believe in myself. You will always be very near and dear to my heart. I can't thank you enough for your guidance, wisdom and support.

The decision to publish has taken me over a year filled with days of solitude and deep soul searching that forced me to seek answers to questions that could sway my decision one way or the other. Why would I publish? What do I hope to gain? There will be positive and negative reactions; Will I be ready to rip off the Band-Aid and expose my wounds? Am I strong enough to carry the wrath?

The reasons for sharing my personal journey as a birth mother are twofold. First, I wanted to write what I couldn't find. What I mean by that is that when I started my search for my daughter, I was desperate to find resources to help me cope emotionally. To be honest I didn't know what I was looking for.

I just wanted to connect with someone, anyone who shared a similar heartbreak. Walking away from your newborn, leaving her alone in a hospital surrounded by strangers, is a horrible, traumatic, life-altering experience. It strips you of your identity and you are *never* who you once were. The mirror became a reflection of an indescribable brokenness that only I could see and feel. I couldn't connect with anything I found on bookshelves, YouTube or self-help videos. I felt alone in a judgmental world and prayed any decisions I made going forward in my search were for all the right reasons, not selfish ones.

The second reason is to talk about the deep-rooted challenges associated with poverty, alcoholism and mental illness. I jokingly say that every family has some degree of dysfunction; if not we'd all be pretty damn perfect. Our childhood was far from perfect. The roots go deep and were seeded long before I was born so I felt it was important to start my journey with Dad, who was born in 1939 into a large, loving, close-knit family of sixteen brothers and sisters; how he and Mom met, his struggle with alcoholism, the mental impact it had on his family and the role it played in my decision to place my baby for adoption.

Marnie said that my story can help more than just birth mothers surviving the same experience but also those with an alcoholic parent and/or spouse. If I could help just one person see light on his or her darkest days, to give a glimmer of hope, then I had to share my story. I am taking you on this journey because I seek to be understood, I seek to forgive, I seek forgiveness.

To Joey's family: please forgive me if my story upsets you. That was not my intent. There are facts that need to be told in order to portray an accurate picture of our struggles, including those associated with alcoholism. Joey was the love of my life. He was my best friend.

To Dad's surviving siblings, you know I love and adore each and every one of you. Forgive me if you read anything offensive within these pages. I didn't write this with the intent to hurt anyone or to destroy the kind, sweet side of my dad, your brother, because Lord knows he had a huge heart and a smile that lit up a room. I pray that you see this story for what it was intended to portray: addiction not only affects the addict but the entire family. I love my dad and count my blessings every day for the last ten sober years we had together. They were beautiful! It's because of our relationship during those last ten years that I am confident his advice to me would be, "It is what it is, honey. You can't change the truth. This is your story to tell." Dad, if you're looking down on me, I love you and hope you are nodding your head in agreement.

Mom, you were instrumental in helping me document a time before I existed. Your ability to recall every little detail, at eighty years of age, astounds me considering I barely remember what I did yesterday. Your life was not easy, Mom, and I don't blame you for the decisions *I* made. Your burdens were heavy, and knowing I added to the load has always been a bitter pill for me to swallow. I realized that digging a grave deep enough to bury my shame was futile because the ghosts from my past will forever haunt me. I've said this to you before but it's worth repeating: "I am a strong woman because a strong woman raised me." Thank you for encouraging me to tell my story and for your blessing to publish it. You are my hero. I adore and love you more than words can express.

To my beautiful daughters, Charlene and Krystal, I thank the higher powers for blessing me with the gift of being your mom and a grandmother who is insanely in love with your babies. Thank you for supporting me through all the crazy moments in our lives that turned into beautiful memories.

Thank you for brightening my darkest days by saying, "Don't worry Mommy, everything will be OK." Thank you for understanding that writing and sharing my story has been a healing journey for me. You are my sunshine; I am who I am because of you. I love you.

To my surviving siblings, Tammy, Billy, Fred and Craig. I internalized my sadness and feelings for over twenty years. I didn't talk to anyone about my experience until I started searching for my daughter because, as independent as I am, I knew this was probably the one journey I couldn't walk alone. Starting the conversation wasn't easy but when I did, I quickly learned that you always had my back and that your love was always and forever will be unconditional. I should have known better and trusted you more. We stuck together during some rough times and are better human beings because of it. Supporting and encouraging me to write my story is the best gift you could ever give me.

Ralph, my husband, my love! Thank you for loving me, flaws and all, and for taking a chance on proposing when I was adamant I would never marry again. You embraced this large, crazy and chaotic family of mine. Then I tell you I'm going to write a book and oh, by the way, try to keep the house tidy because you know a messy house causes me great stress! Thank you for doing the laundry, the dishes, cooking, cleaning and the shopping while I locked myself away for months to write. However, that did free you up to watch more sports, so I guess it was a win-win situation! You reassured me constantly that you would do whatever it took to help me see this through to the end and you haven't once wavered.

When I was stuck on a book title you said, "Why not name it after the poem you wrote, *Does She Think of Me*? I connected with it immediately. It is perfect! Working all day and writing all night caused me to be a cranky bear some days—well, let's be honest here, most days! Not to mention writing about my experience as a birth mother was extremely mentally and emotionally draining. Thank you for your patience and support. I am beyond blessed to have you and your children, Elizabeth and Robert, in my life. Thank you for choosing *me* to be your life partner. I love you, you are my rock, my twin flame, my soulmate.

To Kelly's parents, Diane and Wayne (now deceased), as well as her brothers, Bryan and Shayne, thank you for sharing her with me, for trusting that I would never abandon her again. I so desperately wanted her to have more happy childhood memories than bad. Placing my child for adoption held no guarantees that she would have a perfect childhood and/or a perfect life. But I knew, deep into the depths of my soul, that if another mother chose my child, she would be blessed with more than I could have ever given her. I prayed she would have everything I didn't and nothing of what I lived through. You gave her the life in my dreams and so much more. I am eternally grateful for your love and support, and for your family accepting me and mine into yours.

My dearest sweet Kelly. Waiting eighteen years to find out if you were OK, if you had a good life and if you were happy was the most painful, tormenting journey I've ever travelled on. When I started searching for you, I prepared myself for the worst, but hearing you say, "You made the right decision," gave me permission to heal. My world is less broken knowing you have a wonderful family who gave you a childhood very different from the one your birth father, Joey, and I could have ever given you. Allowing me to be a part of your life is more than I could have ever prayed for. Thank you for accepting me and allowing me to love you. Most importantly, thank you for forgiving me.

To my dad. There was a time when I cried for the childhood we didn't have and was angry when your addiction intermittently turned our worlds upside down. I had a love-hate relationship with you. At times I hated that I loved you and other times I loved that I hated you. There is one thing I am so grateful for though: my last ten years with you sober allowed me the opportunity to let you know that you taught me what love was by being the first to say, "I love you." Yes, saying it when you were intoxicated had no meaning, but I am so grateful for the days when it did. I miss our daily phone calls and managed to save a voicemail message of yours that goes like this, "Hey Cack, it's just the old hobo calling. Love you and God Bless."

Thank you, dad, for teaching me that love endures all. Last but not least thank you to anyone and everyone who has ever said to me, "You have to write a book."

Does she think of me?

She looks in the mirror and asks, who do I see?
A mirage of questions staring back at me.
My hair, my eyes, the colour of my skin
do I resemble any of my kin?
Does she think of me?

Someone out there must know
answers to these questions I ask as I grow.
My laugh, my smile, my walk
Do I sound like another when I talk?
Does she think of me?

I'm sensitive, loving and caring, it shows.
My personality and mannerisms nobody knows.
From where it all came or with whom do I share
these characteristics, does anyone care?
I wonder, does she ever think of me?

★ ★ ★

She's had her first tooth, walked her first walk,
said her first words, as she learned how to talk.
Another's hand guided her safely across the road,
"Obey all the signs," she was lovingly told.
Does she think of me?

I bet she's learned how to ride her first bike,
Sang her first song on her Fisher Price mic.
Raided the closet, make-up to find
for dressing up was so divine.
Does she think of me?

Does She Think of Me

Her first day of school, was she happy or sad?
Oh my, the friends she must have had.
Childhood diseases, which ones did she catch?
Chickenpox are the worst because of the itch.
Does she think of me?

The years have flown so quickly now.
So many questions, I need answers somehow.
Is she dating, does she drive a car?
Is she out on her own? To get to her, is it far?
But most of all, does she ever think of me?

Your cake this year, twenty candles will hold.
Twenty years of pain, for me, will slowly unfold.
What had seemed impossible is finally here
as I gently touch your cheek so fair.
The answer to my question is plain to see,
I no longer have to ask: Does she think of me?

Prologue

September 24, 1979

"You're making a very selfless and brave decision," said the soft-spoken, dark-haired social worker as she slowly slid the documents onto the cold overbed table positioned across my lap.

Glancing down at the document, Joey's and my mother's names were staring back at me. If giving our baby a name was the only privilege we were granted then she should be named after the strongest women we know, her grandmothers, Juanita Clotilda Williams. At the bottom of the page was an "X" next to the signature line. A wave of hopelessness slammed through my body with the impact of a freight train. I never felt more alone than I did in that moment, knowing my signature was the final act to relinquishing my baby girl.

Relinquish, there's a word. Why don't they just say it for what it is? You're giving away your baby, you cruel, heartless bitch. As if she was a hand-me-down, something I had outgrown. Bravery had absolutely nothing to do with it!

Sitting on the side of the firm hospital bed, my feet resting on the cold floor, painful aftereffects of childbirth overtook me. The cold, sterile hospital room started spinning out of control. Everything around me was being forcefully sucked into the dark vortex of despair. My unseen child was ripped from my body and forced into the swirling unknown along with the fragments of whatever was left of my broken soul. The adoption papers, my baby, my heart all sucked into the dark, spinning abyss.

The noise of the crackling plastic-covered mattress broke the deafening quiet as I slowly lowered my broken body back into bed. Curled up in a fetal position, I wrapped my arms around the spare pillow, now suctioned to my chest, and sobbed until I could barely breathe. An unexpected commotion startled me into shameful silence. The punishment for my heartless action would soon become painfully clear.

An aged, light blue, drooping drape with missing hooks was all that separated our two very different worlds. She was exhausted from childbirth, but adrenaline prevented her from sleeping. Lying on my side facing her bed, the sounds of her baby suckling at her breast emanated through the woven fibers of the washed-out drape. The sounds triggered my body to feed an infant I would never hold. My breast felt wet and cold. I hugged the sterile pillow tighter to my chest as the tears slowly rolled down my cheeks. In that moment of cruel existence, I wanted to die.

I was begrudgingly envious of that mom, the fragrant pink flowers, the tiny doll-sized gifts, and the swarm of visitors that joyfully danced past the foot of my tear-stained bed. There was nowhere to hide but under the rough, stiff flannel blanket that offered little comfort. Burying my head under my pillow to block out their joy, I prayed they were oblivious to my agony.

For four days we shared a room but never spoke. I hid behind the faded blue curtain. Our silence a confession of my guilt.

As the sun was going down, the torturous sounds of the day fell silent, resting up for another performance at dawn.

Darkness made way for gut-wrenching demons of sleepless shame and guilt.

A calm fell over the nurses' station with the exception of one haunting infant cry echoing through the halls of the maternity ward. With every annoying tick-tock of the clock on the wall, I dreaded for morning to come, not only for the unwanted sounds of new moms with their babies that caused me *so much* pain but for my discharge. My God, how would I find the strength to leave her behind?

My thoughts were suddenly redirected to that haunting cry vibrating along the walls of the sleepy maternity ward. It was hypnotizing. The longer I listened the more I realized the unhappy cry was coming from the nursery. The powerful hypnotic force controlled me as I painfully inched my way to a sitting position at the side of the bed. *Am I losing my mind? Is that crying infant calling me?*

I stood at the door of my room and peeked out into the dimly-lit hallway. I hesitated. The nasty nurse from the operating room saying, "You will not be permitted to see your baby at birth," replayed over and over in my mind. *Should I go? Oh my God, if I'm caught near the nursery what will happen to me?* Pushing through the fear, I carefully set one foot in front of the other to minimize the sound of my hard-soled slippers on the polished floor. All other moms and babies were fast asleep except two. Me and that crying infant!

The nurses' station was unattended. I stared at the blue sign hung on the cream-coloured, chipped walls and cautiously followed the arrow pointing in the direction of the nursery. The baby's cries became louder the closer I got. My heart banged in my ears. I was beyond the point of no return; I just had to see that baby! Destiny controlled the reins and I was convinced that this was meant to be. God help the person who tried to stop me.

Pausing at the entrance of the nursery I observed a nurse holding the tiniest bottle of formula I had ever seen and gently rocking a wailing infant tightly swaddled in a stiff white flannel blanket with stripes on the end. The dim light fixture on the wall shone down on her tiny body. As I entered the room, I made eye contact with the nurse for a brief second, and immediately turned my attention to the baby in her arms. "Is this baby Williams?" were the only words that squeaked past what felt like a softball in my throat. "Yes," she said softly with a warm smile, unaware of who I was and unprepared for what was about to unfold.

Crying inconsolably just moments before, the baby girl fell quiet at the sound of my voice as if knowing her momma was there. She was unaware that her silence would give me the strength to do what I needed to. Wiping the tears from my eyes, I took a mental picture of the moment that was denied me when she left the safety of my womb and took her first breath. I looked at my baby for the first—and what could potentially be the last—time. A flood of emotions washed over me. Fear, shame and guilt rolled down my cheeks and onto her chest as I cupped her face in my shaking hand. She was so tiny, so soft and for a brief moment, still mine. Leaning into her, my lips touching her soft, warm, fuzzy forehead, I inhaled the newness of her. Wishing this moment was secretly ours, I whispered, "Please remember that I will always love you. Please forgive me."

I was too afraid to make eye contact with the nurse that was holding her but there was an air of paralysis in the room. Naïve and consumed with fear that she would call security, I conjured up every ounce of strength I had, turned and slowly left the nursery. She didn't call security. She let me have my moment. A mental picture, captured in a few precious moments, would sustain me for the next eighteen years until I could legally start searching for her. As I walked away, it was *my* broken cries that vibrated down the corridor.

Chapter 1

Who in their right mind would give birth to seventeen children? Single births, no twins, no pain medication. Heck, I had one child and swore I'd never do that again. I believe the word I used was "barbaric."

My paternal grandmother, lovingly referred to as Nan, lived in a time when birth control was illegal and punishable by law. Women accepted the pain of childbirth as their purpose in life, so by the age of forty-four in 1959, my Nan had given birth to seventeen children. Think about it: she barely had time to heal from the trauma of childbirth before finding herself expecting again. I'm doing the math and—holy cow!—she would have been pregnant for approximately seventeen years. Unfathomable!

Nan lost two children shortly after childbirth, and a twenty-six-year-old son in a horrific car crash. Soft spoken, gentle and unassuming, Nan was a heavy-set lady who suffered from a condition called dropsy, an old term for fluid buildup in the legs, ankles and feet. Some even referred to it as "elephant legs." Today it would be classified as edema due to congestive heart failure. Many women risked their mental and physical health, some even their lives, with annual pregnancies. Nan was no exception.

Seventeen children, a couple of players shy of a hockey team, was most likely the furthest thing from Poppy's mind when he built their tiny three-bedroom home from his hard-earned income as a seasonal labourer. The small grey clapboard dwelling was located on Forest Pond Road, named after the serene pond located across the road from his home, in the township of the Goulds. Like a Rockwell painting, Forest Pond was nestled in a valley surrounded by rolling hills, grassy fields and mature trees.

With no plumbing, the main water supply was hauled in five-gallon buckets by hand from a man-made well. A closet was converted into a bathroom that contained a chamber pot and a five-gallon bucket that served as a toilet. When that was full of human waste it had to be taken to the pit behind the house and dumped. Sponge baths were taken behind the cardboard walls that divided the house into rooms. The one light bulb dangling from the ceiling with a pull chain provided lighting but wasn't always reliable. It flickered on and off with each yank of the chain until one final pull provided a steady stream of light.

The long, cold, harsh winters whistled through the rafters six to seven months of the year. The hand-crafted wooden box, near the heavy black cast iron range-top stove, was well stocked with firewood that provided the fuel for cooking and was the only source of heat for the entire house. It took a strong back to chop down and haul trees with nothing but a rope and calloused hands as tough as leather. The trees were chopped into just the right size chunks to fit into the wood burning stove and stacked strategically with space for air to circulate, allowing the wood to dry. Special care was taken to not burn green (wet) wood because a black, sticky, tar-like substance called creosote would build up on the interior of the chimney over time. This could easily ignite into a chimney fire causing the house to burn down.

To extend the supply of firewood, the heat was contained within the kitchen by hanging an old wool blanket on two rusty nails across the archway opening. It was the only room in the house that was heated.

I would have loved to experience mealtime at Nanny and Poppy's. Enquiring minds want to know, seriously "How do you feed seventeen children in a small country kitchen?" In rotation of course, from the youngest to the oldest. Nan always ate last, feeding on the scraps left behind. She always put her family's needs before her own.

The grey and white linoleum flooring was well-worn from the constant shuffling of feet in and out of the house as family and friends entered the kitchen through the back porch. Anything and everything could happen at the kitchen table from baking, to eating, to working on car parts, to singing and dancing over a few drinks—commonly referred to in Newfoundland as a "Kitchen Party." Although Dad only had a Grade 4 education, he was a very talented musician. Self-taught, he could pick up any musical instrument and belt out a tune without a sheet of music. Unfortunately, it took a lot of liquid courage for him to showcase his talent at a Kitchen Party. But when he did, he was Johnny Cash brilliant.

Although a pretty lace valance and half curtain hung in the kitchen window, blankets provided the only means of privacy from the outside world. The kitchen and my grandparents' bedroom were the only two rooms that had drywall and a ceiling, which was constructed of cardboard, old coats and clothing. All other rooms were exposed to the trusses with cardboard walls separating them into private sleeping quarters.

This rural lifestyle wasn't foreign to Newfoundlanders in the 1940s. They never referred to themselves as poor. *Hard times* was the term commonly used when funds and food were low. Daily routines were structured around work, chores and raising families. Growing your own vegetables, hunting for moose and rabbits, as well as catching and salting codfish were pivotal to survival. Hand-knit socks, sweaters, mittens and scarves kept you warm in the cold months. When hand-me-down clothes had made their rounds, they were cut into squares and sewn into a quilt. Nothing was wasted.

Although people complained about nosey neighbours peering out from behind closed curtains, there was a sense of comfort in knowing those prying eyes would detect if anything was amiss. Veering off script from daily routine could warrant a phone call from the neighbour to see if everyone was OK. If your curtains stayed drawn all day and you didn't answer your phone, well, let's just say, your next of kin were called to check in on you.

Here we are in the twenty-first century living in cookie-cutter houses built so close together, imprisoning us behind our closed blinds and drawn curtains. Do we know our neighbours' routines? Would we know if they were in trouble? Probably not.

Our lives have become so automated that the thought of not having a dishwasher, washer, dryer, shower, flushing toilets, and heat thermostatically controlled in every room of the house might be grounds for divorce. Hanging laundry on a clothesline all year round, chopping wood and taking sponge baths in a cold room in winter is not my idea of a good time. If I had to pick between sitting on a five-gallon bucket to relieve myself or making a trip to a smelly, spider-infested outhouse in the middle of the night, the bucket would be the throne of choice. Let's not get stupid here. Although I long for simpler times, it will not be at the expense of a comfy bathroom with running water and flushing toilets.

Chapter 2

It was love at first sight. They had met at a friend's birthday party the year prior. He was a handsome brute of a man, standing 6'6" with a thick head of dark wavy hair and piercing blue eyes that sparkled above a mischievous grin. Although he embodied a chick magnet combination of Johnny Cash and Elvis Presley, only one girl at the party caught his eye. Her thick, blazing red locks were neatly held in place by a floral bandana that he playfully tugged at. Their eyes met as she slowly readjusted her bandana, sending his heart a flutter. Her cheeks flushed as she shied away from his good looks and irresistible charm. With every sideways glance she flashed in his direction, he feared his heart would pound out of his chest. From that day on they were inseparable. That is, until the day he accepted a job as a heavy equipment operator 1600 kilometres away at the Canadian Forces Base in Happy Valley-Goose Bay, Labrador. Lack of employment forced many Newfoundlanders to leave the island in search of work and a better life.

Handwritten love letters or a weekly phone call from the communal pay phone was the only means of communication in the 1950s. No email, text messages or Facetime. Line-ups were long, conversations were romantically limp, public, short and cordial. Could their love survive a long-distance relationship?

Mom's cousin, Sophie, who lived in Labrador as well, concocted a plan to have Mom flown to Labrador to be her live-in babysitter. Making up the little white lie was the easy part. Convincing Mom's mother to let her go would be a whole other kettle of fish. My maternal Nan was a strict lady who ruled the home with an iron fist. If my husband passed away at fifty-two years of age leaving me to raise seven kids on my own, I would too. Everyone had chores and, when old enough, worked to help with the finances. The chances she would allow Mom, a source of income, to go to Labrador were slim to none. But for some unknown reason, Nan said yes.

Mom arrived in Labrador, not as Sophie's live-in babysitter but as a billeting housekeeper on the United States Armed Forces Base. Billeting was a term used for temporary accommodations for airmen who landed at the Emergency Alert Base to refuel and rest for a night or two. As a housekeeper Mom worked long, hard hours but, at the end of the day she was in the arms of the man she was destined to spend the rest of her life with. That made everything OK.

Of all the days to pick for a wedding, April 1, 1960 may have been the worst. It was a cold, blustery, snowy afternoon in Labrador. I'm not superstitious but if I were, snow on your wedding day could mean either a stormy marriage or good luck for happiness, wealth and fertility. Either way it's the luck of the draw, I guess. Did guests attend the April Fool's Day wedding to witness the joining of two people in holy matrimony or were they holding their breath waiting for the prank to be revealed? As the day unfolded, the chosen path was anything but a joke.

The old white clapboard-covered church was surrounded by snow as white as the lace wedding dress draped over her trembling body. With every step she relived the precious moments that delivered her to this day. Joy consumed her as she paused at the double wooden doors. She couldn't be any happier than she was in that moment. Grinning from ear to ear, a vision of innocence and purity in a full-length, long-sleeved white gown she had purchased from the Sears catalogue, she entered and slowly made her way to the altar. Her blazing red hair beamed through the shear waist-length veil that covered her freckled, fair-skinned face. Each methodically paced, graceful step echoed off the walls of the cold, empty, musty church.

Their two best friends as witnesses and the minister stood at the altar for the private ceremony. Butterflies fluttering in her stomach were now replaced with nausea and panic as she realized her groom was absent. The delicate white shoes on her feet felt like cement as she realized their best friends didn't know his whereabouts either. *Where was he? Did he get cold feet? How long do we wait?* With every passing minute the minister grew more and more restless and threatened to leave if the groom was much later.

Jim, the best man, stepped forward offering to marry her and raise her unborn child as his own. She'd known for a long time that Jim had a crush on her. She admired him but not enough to marry him, especially since she was carrying another man's child. Before she could respond, in stumbled the groom, thirty minutes late and drunk. If she wasn't carrying his child, she might have left him at the altar, but she didn't; she loved him enough to stay. In front of her witnesses, she vowed to take him as her husband, for better or worse, for richer or poorer, in sickness and health, to love and to cherish until death parted them.

Three hundred guests welcomed Mr. and Mrs. Arthur Williams into the reception hall. She was beaming, immersed in every speech and toast to the happy couple. As the drunk groom became more and more intoxicated, rumours were spreading amongst the guests that he would not have the ability to make it through their first dance. The alcohol flowing through his veins made him bold and cocky. Proving the audience wrong, he swept her off her feet and danced the never-ending dance. In that moment she was happier than she had ever been. She wanted this feeling to last forever.

The party continued into the evening and at the stroke of midnight, as tradition goes, the bride and groom were to leave for their honeymoon. He was nowhere to be found. Earlier he told a friend that he was heading back to the hotel and staggered out into the dark, stormy night. Thinking her groom was at the hotel, the embarrassed bride left the reception alone and arrived at an empty honeymoon suite. She lay on the bed waiting for him to return, yearning to be released from the virgin white gown, to feel his hands on her body. Visions of her perfect honeymoon drifted off into the darkness leaving her feeling abandoned for the second time on her wedding day.

Thirty-nine beautiful silk-covered buttons flowed from the neck to the waist of her white lace gown. Unable to reach them, she was imprisoned with no way to slip out of what had become a bittersweet memory. At three o'clock in the morning she awoke and made her way to the shared bathroom just outside their hotel room. It was there she asked a complete stranger to undo the thirty-nine silk covered buttons.

A loud knock on the door shortly after sunrise jolted her to her feet. Her disheveled husband, standing there with the police, had no topcoat and no shoelaces. Drunk and disorderly charges on their honeymoon night landed him in jail. Just twenty-four hours prior she had placed a wedding band on the fourth finger of his left hand, the finger closest to the heart. The shiny gold band was gone and never recovered.

Shortly after their wedding, Dad purchased a used shed made from plywood and scraps of wood from a nearby construction site. Used to lock up tools and materials, you would never dream of living in one, but that's what they did. He added an extension, put in an artesian well and called it home-sweet-home just in time for the arrival of their first child.

With the early onset of labour and no phone, the nearest neighbour with a car was a twenty-minute walk in -30°C weather. With every contraction that slowed her down she feared more and more her baby would be born in the dark of night on a pile of frozen leaves at the side of the road.

They finally made it to the neighbour's place and he rushed them to the hospital. Upon arrival she was whisked away to deliver their baby alone, without the support of her husband.

Having a baby was considered a female event. Fathers were ushered to smoke-filled waiting rooms close enough to the labour and delivery rooms in earshot of their wives crying out in pain. They patiently and nervously awaited the nurse to announce the safe arrival of their child.

"Congratulations," the nurse said, holding a baby so tightly wrapped she looked like a sausage. "You're the proud father of a bouncing baby girl." On October 20, 1960, my sister Tammy was born. She weighed-in at a whopping 11.5 pounds and had a full head of blazing red hair just like her mom.

I thought having my first child with no epidural was scary and barbaric. I couldn't imagine going through that with strangers. How times have changed. Now you can have as many people as you want in the delivery room, within reason of course.

Tammy was five months old when Dad got word his mother's heart was failing. She was dying. Described as an angel on Earth, it was apparent that his mom was adored not for what she took but for what she gave. He loved her more than life itself, so returning to Newfoundland wasn't an option, it was a must. With no financial means to travel, he feared he might never see her alive again. He longed to give her one final kiss and to tell her he loved her one last time.

Dad was a giver not a receiver. He would rather give you the shirt off his back then to receive assistance, but desperation sent him to the only person who wouldn't judge him: the minister of their church. Psalm 34:17 says, "When the righteous cry for help, the Lord heard and delivered them out of all their troubles." The minister responded to Dad's cry for help and offered him the money.

Would he make it in time? Will he get to say one final goodbye? He prayed for God to deliver him home in time as he packed the bare necessities. Standing at his mother's bedside his prayers were answered as he gave her one final kiss goodbye and told her he loved her. She passed away in March of 1961 at the age of fifty-two, leaving behind five daughters still living at home. The youngest, my Aunt Marjorie, was eight years of age. I was born six months later and never met my Nan, but I have learned, from memories shared, that she was larger than life. Her legacy was love, woven into each of her children's DNA before they were even born. Every thread that binds this family together is intertwined with stories of sacrifice, unconditional love, hardship and survival.

With five sisters now without a mother, Dad knew he had to remain in Newfoundland to help his father raise them. Owing the church money weighed heavy on his mind. The only thing he had of any monetary value was his house in Labrador, so he transferred the property deed to the minister as repayment for the outstanding debt. A close friend in Labrador packed and shipped all their worldly possessions to them, including their wedding gifts, which fit into two large travel trunks.

My three brothers, Billy, Craig and Darren were born eleven months apart. Twelve people now lived in a small three-bedroom home. With no ceilings in all but two rooms and cardboard for insulation, winter nights were brutally cold. I saw white frost on the rusty nail heads as I looked up at the rafters from my bed.

Every household that relied on wood as a source of heat stoked their stoves with hardwood before crawling under the security of a heavy quilt. Hardwood is slow burning and produces more heat than softer wood. But Dad's father feared fires and refused to keep the stove lit at night. Hence, Mom dressed us in our snowsuits over our pajamas and covered us with heavy handmade quilts. The heaviest, warmest quilts were those made from discarded wool army uniforms. Itchy but warm.

Today, heavy quilts have been redesigned and are now known as weighted or gravity blankets. Sleeping under a weighted blanket apparently releases what's called "happiness hormones." I find this so ironic that a handmade item of necessity that kept us from freezing to death in the 1960s has been proven to relieve stress and make a person happy. Go figure!

Mrs. Cummings, Mom's best friend, asked her to babysit her three kids for two weeks so she could vacation with her husband on the boats where he worked. Mom agreed on the condition that she could bring her wringer washer with her to keep ahead of the laundry eight kids would produce. I chuckle as I try to envision Mom, the babysitter, arriving with five kids and pushing a squeaky, rusty, pot-bellied washing machine ahead of her.

Two days later, on October 9, 1967 while trying to settle into a routine with eight kids, Dad's father's house burned to the ground. I was only six, but I remember looking out the big bay window to see monstrous red flames engulfing our home.

People formed a bucket brigade that ran from the pond, up across the road and onto the lawn attempting to get as close to the burning timbers as possible. The heavy buckets of water were passed swiftly from one exhausted sweaty person to the next. The cardboard-fueled fire roared louder at their efforts and danced in the reflection of everyone's panic-stricken eyes as they stared helplessly into its hypnotic glow.

Dad braved the burning house twice in an attempt to rescue the three people left inside. He found the lifeless bodies of his father and his cousin, Albert, and managed to push them out a back window onto the ground below. The fire forced him out before he could find his two-year-old nephew, Walter. Dad never talked about it, but I know he blamed himself for not saving that precious little boy.

Twelve of us lived in that house but there were only three at home the night of the fire. If Mom hadn't agreed to help Mrs. Cummings, we may have all perished in that inferno as well.

The flames spewed sparks onto the two homes next door that belonged to Dad's siblings forcing them to evacuate. Neighbouring family and friends opened their doors to offer a safe haven to approximately thirty adults and children.

The cause of the fire was never determined. Could it have been the faulty light dangling from the ceiling? Was it a chimney fire or could it have been an innocent child playing with matches? Ironically, the element Poppy feared the most, fire, was the very thing that ended his life.

Chapter 3

After the devastating fire, Dad moved us into a house trailer that had no plumbing, no running water or electricity, and no telephone. We hadn't lived there very long when Dad's sister announced she was moving her family to Montreal, so he bought their small two-bedroom home located next door to where his father's house once stood. The only access to running water was via a hand-operated pump located in the kitchen. There was a bathroom of sorts, in that there was a porcelain toilet that didn't function, but it was way more comfortable than sitting on a rough-rimmed pail. To flush the contents into the septic tank, buried deep underground at the front of the house, required dumping a bucket of water into the toilet. It was more of a manual process but much better than dragging a bucket of human waste to the pit and emptying it, praying all the while you didn't slop any of the smelly contents on you.

We still relied on a cast iron, oil and wood range (stove) for heat. When the nights got colder Mom pulled out the old wool blankets and hung them in the doorway to once again keep the heat contained to the kitchen.

We hauled water from the well and poured it into the aluminum warming vessel attached to the back of the black cast iron stove. Then, we employed a large dipper to scoop up the warm water and fill the large aluminum laundry wash tub that, when perched atop two chrome chairs, also served as a bathtub.

Mom had bath time down to a science, starting with the youngest and finishing with the oldest. "Don't throw the baby out with the bathwater," was a phrase I heard often as a child. By the time the last child was bathed the water was soapy and murky leaving me to believe a child could go unseen and risk being thrown out with the bathwater. I chuckle now knowing that phrase had nothing to do with throwing out a baby.

Saturdays were predictable and routine. Kids were up, dressed, fed and sent outside to play. We followed our curiosities and disappeared for a few hours to explore the neighbourhood. Although we never had adult supervision, we knew every neighbour in the area would report back to Mom if we were seen doing anything out of line. We walked barefoot, danced in the rain, climbed trees and swam in nearby lakes. This gave Mom three or four hours to focus on chores.

She would make a batch of bread, cook a huge pot of pea soup with dumplings and tackle the house cleaning. Bed linens and laundry were washed in the round, pot-bellied wringer washer. The squeaky agitators worked the clothes clean, then they were put through the wringers to squeeze out the soapy water and then dropped into the aluminum tub filled with clean rinse water. She rinsed the clothes and rung them out by hand to extract as much water as possible before putting them through the wringers again. She repeated this process until all the laundry was on the clothesline in the backyard. Once dry, they were folded and put away.

The winter months were unbearable as she continued to hang the clothes on the line rain or snow without fail. You could barely feel the clothespins between your fingers it was so cold. But Mom loved to wake on a Saturday morning to a beautiful, sunny windy day. "Some day on clothes, Dot!" she would yell to her sister-in-law next door, as she carried a basket filled with heavy, wet clothes across the backyard to the clothesline. Between washing, rinsing and hanging out clothes, Mom managed to prepare lunch, feed us and send us back out to play. "There's no rest for the weary," she would say.

Having lived through that era and been tasked with doing laundry as soon as I could reach the washer, I have an appreciation for the convenience of automatic washers and dryers today.

I don't feel like 1971 was that long ago, but when I talk about wringer washers and flannel diapers, I feel ancient. Heck, we had recycling down to a science before it became a buzz word. Five-gallon buckets were used for everything: to haul water, for toilets, and they were blueberry receptacles during berry picking season. No, the bucket used as a toilet was not the one used for storing blueberries! Oh, we also soaked soiled flannel diapers in them to rinse the poop off before they were put through the washing machine. My sister and I inherited that nasty little task.

It's odd how certain memories escape us and others we can't forget. To this day, if I smell Ivory Snow laundry detergent, I am transported back to 1971, when I was nine years old, standing in front of a five-gallon bucket filled with cold water and poopy diapers. To this day I can still envision how soft the flannel cloth felt in my hands as I twisted the clean fabric tight forcing the water to squish through my tiny fingers.

My youngest brother, Fred, was the last addition to the family. Arriving ten years after me, we refer to him as the "oops" baby. To accommodate our large family Dad built an extension onto the house that became a master bedroom where Fred also slept as a baby. A double cast iron squeaky bed with an old, soft, comfy mattress was in the second bedroom where five of us kids slept. My sister and I lay at the top and the three boys at the bottom. That would definitely be shunned upon today.

With the kitchen sealed off during the winter months, the bedrooms were freezing cold. To warm up our bed Mom heated chunks of wood in the oven, wrapped them in towels and placed them between the sheets. The smell of burning wood takes me back to five shivering kids in winter, scurrying to get under the heavy quilts, their feet desperately searching in the dark for the hot spot that embraces their soul with so much more than just warmth; it was a mother's love.

We lived in that tiny house for five years. For four of those years, Dad was building a new, much larger, three-bedroom home on his father's property next door. When we moved in, my four brothers shared a bedroom with bunk beds and my sister and I shared another. It was an odd feeling not having five bodies in one bed providing warmth on cold nights, but the reality was we didn't need it because we now had electricity.

I'm a deep thinker and my mind goes places it sometimes shouldn't, like the hardships, trials and tribulations we lived through. Were they a curse? Were they inflicted on us by a tragic memory buried deep beneath the ashes on which we lived? I am not a cardholder of any religious organization, but I do believe there is a higher power somewhere out there, way too big for me to comprehend or assign definition to. Would it have been comforting to know that the property where three family members died was blessed and sprinkled with holy water before our new home was erected there? Maybe, but knowing it hadn't leaves me asking questions I will never know the answers to.

Chapter 4

Beautiful Italian lace, silks and satins dressed the big bay windows that overlooked the manicured lawn of the huge mansions on Cornwall Heights in St. John's. The upper class lived there, and Mom and her friend would go to admire, of all things, window coverings. The drapery elegantly hung with pretty tiebacks that held them open during the day revealing little view of the inside. The only commonality between their world and ours were shadows behind closed drapes. Nothing more, just shadows.

"Close da curtains," Mom would say in her strong Newfoundland accent as the sun went down. It was our cue to switch on the lights. "Ya don't want the neighbours gawkin' in at us."

Dark memories that cause us the most pain latch on like bloodsucking leeches. They drain our souls leaving us desperately clinging onto what is perceived as normal. Alcohol owned my dad's soul. It dictated every aspect of our lives. It defined us. It was all we knew. Alcohol was the dark ugly shadow lurking behind *our* curtains. It was *our* normal.

Dad was a heavy, episodic drinker with binges lasting anywhere from a few weeks to a couple of months. The uncertainty was not in whether the behaviour would repeat itself but when. Intoxication spiraled him into uncontrollable bouts of crying, and erratic, unpredictable mood swings. Although Dad never raised his voice or a hand to us, the emotional blows as a result of his addiction caused us low self-esteem and depression, as well as challenges performing academically. Five of his six kids were high school dropouts.

I learned to not take Dad's sober days for granted because they would soon be followed by a long alcoholic binge. Sober Dad worked as a heavy equipment operator on construction sites in the summer and as a snowplough operator in the winter. He was admired for his precise talent with monster size equipment that most of us would find cumbersome. Colleagues were in awe of how close he fearlessly dug to a gas line, never puncturing one.

Newfoundland weather is very unpredictable. A beautiful sunny day can change to fog and rain in the blink of an eye. This is why Newfoundlanders often say, "If you don't like the weather, just wait five minutes." In 1978, the year I became pregnant, 569.3 centimeters (nineteen feet) of snow fell. To put that into perspective, the average height of a utility pole was twenty feet. With that much snow on the roads most heavy equipment operators would do one pass with the snowplough, leaving motorists with a treacherous "cow path" to maneuver through. It wasn't in Dad's nature to follow the behaviours of others. For example, he made the news one year when he used the snowplough blade to toss an abandoned car to the top of a snowbank. I felt very proud to overhear neighbours say, "Art must have cleared the roads because they are wide enough for two lanes of traffic to get through."

Everyone's definition of *normal* varies. Dad's sobriety defined our *normal*. My sweetest memories are of Saturday mornings. The aroma of pea soup with dumplings simmering on the stove and homemade bread baking in the oven wafted through the open windows. Music of the 50s serenaded all activities with tunes from Kitty Wells, Patsy Cline, Jim Reeves and, of course, Johnny Cash. Just thinking of it brings me a sense of calm, peace and security.

Dad took us to church Sunday mornings while Mom stayed home and prepared Jiggs dinner, a traditional Sabbath meal promptly served at noon. In Newfoundland, dinner means lunch, supper means dinner, and an evening snack is lunch. I know, confusing, right?

As long as eight seats around the wooden dinner table had bums in them, life was *normal*. Singing was not proper at the table and Dad made sure we never left our seat without thanking Mom for the meal she prepared. Everyone would help clean up the kitchen then all eight of us would pile into the car for a Sunday afternoon drive. By today's standards Dad would have received a hefty ticket for seatbelt violations. Two adults in the front with the youngest child on Mom's lap and five of us in the back with not a seatbelt to be found.

Five kids confined to the back seat would just about kill each other, but the threat of no ice cream if we continued to bicker were the magic words to keep us quiet. So, we sat patiently, listening to music from the cassette tape player that was randomly interrupted with Mom saying, "Oh my, look at those beautiful curtains."

Sunday afternoon drives were usually about an hour long to visit relatives we didn't get to see very often. We arrived to open arms, big squishy hugs, fresh baked treats and the large aluminum kettle whistling on the black cast iron stove top.

Kids were seen and not heard, which meant we were shooed outside to play. Boisterous chatter, jolly laughter and traditional Newfoundland folk music danced past the freshly baked pies cooling on the sill of the open window. Giving myself permission to laugh and enjoy the game of hide-and-seek with my cousins, I filled my lungs with fresh air and exhaled, thankful that life was temporarily ordinary again. As much as I wanted to believe Dad's sobriety would last forever, I learned at an early age that life did not come with guarantees.

Seven bums in seats around the dinner table. The chair at the end, reserved for Dad, was empty. There it was, the elephant in the room. Dinner was always served at 5:00 p.m. and his absence signified the inevitable, he was drinking. I caught Mom nervously glancing at the battery-operated clock on the wall behind me one too many times. The deafening tick-tock, tick-tock, tick-tock broke the silence. We avoided the obvious because it was more comfortable. We pretended everything was *normal* and hoped Dad was delayed for anything other than drinking. Rum was always the reason!

The eye of the storm was approaching. As it picked up speed it viciously sucked us into its cold, dark, swirling centre and slammed us into another world. No one returned unscathed.

★ ★ ★

Burrowing through the three-foot-tall grass, pencil in hand and a pad of unlined white paper tucked under my arm, I picked a spot and fell to the ground. Relying on my senses for comfort, I closed my eyes to feel the warm of the sun on my face and the soothing sound of the grass rustling around me. Curling up in a fetal position I rocked back and forth to the rhythm of the wind.

It's unclear when I realized sketching was a coping mechanism. It swept me away to a world free of worry and uncertainty. I love to smell the printed pages of books and magazines. Although my pad of paper was blank without ink it still had a unique aroma that whisked me away to the land of make-believe. Sketching intricate long flowing velvet robes of witches and wizards I knew fire breathing dragons were not to be feared in a land where delicate fairies playfully danced on the wind. It encased me with a deep sense of calm, a brief distraction from the impending storm.

I had a routine when Dad was drinking. Escape to a magical world buried deep within the tall, green, earth-scented grass. Capture the beauty that lived therein. Pack up my pencils and head back to my not so magical toxic environment. On the days I couldn't escape to the meadows, I'd sit in my room and flip through my sketchpad, to a world of make believe and dream.

Barely able to sit upright on the old wooden chair, his eyes welled with tears as he pulled me onto his swaying knee. "Do you know how much I love you?" rolled off his rum-soaked tongue, dangling on his lips long enough for a tear to scoop it up and splatter it onto the yellow linoleum flooring between his feet. The empty ritualistic response was, "Yes, Dad, I do." Mom would say, "What goes in sober, comes out drunk." I don't know if this meant that, when he was sober, he was too shy to say I love you, but alcohol gave him the courage to express it?

Dad was a smart man and although he only had a Grade 4 education, he successfully started a landscaping and construction business. By that time, he had been sober for four years. Life was great! He showed up every evening of those four years for dinner at exactly 5:00 p.m. until the night he didn't. Dad hit the bottle hard.

He asked his brother-in-law to collect a payment of $29,000 in addition to a case of rum. Dad spent over a week at their home before they called Mom begging her to come get him. Money flowed through his fingers like water as he gambled and drank it all away. Mom never saw a penny of that $29,000.

Everything he worked so hard for came crumbling down around him. Delinquent on payments, he lost his trucks, all his equipment and the business.

For some reason I remember more bad memories of my childhood than good. This particular one is difficult to erase. Dad piled five of us kids, all under the age of eleven, into his double cab pickup truck. I had the sense to know he was drunk but was naïve as to how that would impact his driving abilities. We sat in the back without seatbelts, carefree and excited at the promise of an ice cream cone. Fear was the furthest thing from our minds because, after all, our father wouldn't put us in harm's way. That false sense of security quickly evaporated when he swerved off the road and slid towards a body of water named First Pond. As we were abruptly tossed to one side of the vehicle, I looked up long enough to see the water coming towards us and then felt a sudden jerk. He regained control and managed to get the vehicle back on the road.

Continuing on the narrow, winding road into the small fishing community of Petty Harbour, Dad drove his truck out to the end of the wharf overlooking the calm salty sea. A tear ran down his cheek as he placed both hands on the steering wheel and blankly gazed across the water into the horizon. How heavy do one person's burdens have to get before they morally cross the line into the darkness of no return? Today wasn't the day for him to cross that line. He left the wharf and found himself knocking on the minister's door. "Take them," he cried, gesturing in our direction, "or I'm going to drive them into the ocean."

The burning question I will never know the answer to is: Was the near miss into First Pond intentional with a sudden change of heart? Maybe the water wasn't deep enough to do the job? Maybe driving off the wharf into the deep, cold water of Petty Harbour would have been a better means to an end?

★ ★ ★

The Crystal Palace was a popular bar and nightclub located on the main road in the Goulds and had been around since long before I was born. It was no secret that Dad had a huge heart and would give you the shirt off his back, which is one of the things I loved about him. It came as no surprise to Mom when she received a call from our neighbour, Josey Everard, informing her that Dad was at the Crystal Palace buying rounds for everyone. He had passed out at the bar and his so-called friends were taking the money that was scattered around his head and feet like confetti. Overdue bills, no groceries and six kids to feed fuelled her courage to enter an establishment that prospered on the blood money of ruined lives and families.

Knowing respectable women shouldn't be seen in bars, Josey directed Mom to park her van at the back door and he would escort her in. As she entered the dimly-lit room, she was immediately nauseated by the stench from the smoke-infused dark walls and sticky, beer-stained carpets. Her heart pounded in her ears, drowning out the hail of loud music and drunken chatter as she made her way to her husband's slumped over body. His arms resting on the bar formed a pillow where his head lay. He looked so lost and helpless. It would be a long, dark and lonely road before he got ill enough to beg her for help. She sobered him up many times in the past and knew from experience that this was a decision he had to make on his own, in his own time.

Trembling, she took his wallet, scooped up the bills that lay scattered around his head and feet and turned to face the brightly lit EXIT sign at the other end of the dingy, dark room. Josey guided her through the wall of vulgar obscenities hurled at her by every man she walked past, through to the back door and safely to her van.

Staring at the $3000 laid out on the kitchen table she knew that if it wasn't for Josey that money would have been gambled away or pissed down some filthy urinal. $3000 wasn't near enough money to get her out of the financial mess she was in but for the first time in her life she decided to do something, not out of necessity but just for the hell of it. If other kids in the neighbourhood had bikes, her children would too.

It was a warm, sunny summer's day when, beaming from ear to ear, she pulled into the driveway with shiny new bikes stuffed into her van. Mine was a beautiful, pink, banana-seat bike with shiny pink streamers flowing from each handle grip. She was faster than all their bicycles put together. We no longer looked with envy at the kids who had bikes. We didn't have to sit patiently as they promised to let us have a ride and never did. If I promised to share my bike, I kept my word because I didn't want anyone to ever experience what we did, the feeling of being different.

I guess it was smart thinking on Mom's part because kids on bikes disappear for hours returning only upon hearing the roll call for mealtime. We survived on soups, stews, meat, potatoes, codfish and homemade bread as well as oatmeal, creamed wheat and eggs. Sober Dad loved to hunt, so our freezer was always well stocked with rabbit, moose and caribou. Perched on the front step clad in a faded apron tied tightly around her thick waist, Mom would yell each of our names in a loud Newfoundland accent that echoed across Forest Pond, followed by a long drawn out "IT'S DINNER TIME!"

If her red hair was tucked up under a pair of underwear on her head, serving as a hairnet, you knew there was homemade bread in the makings or a sweet dessert waiting. We helped tidy up after dinner and completed our homework. With six kids, bath time had to be quick, no time for play. The most comforting feeling in the world was slipping into our soft flannel pajamas that had been air dried on the clothesline. Ivory Snow detergent mixed with the fresh outdoor air is not a scent you ever forget.

Staggering home late at night, Dad would wake us up to hand us one small, wrinkled brown paper bag filled with penny candy, beaming as if he'd just given us the world. The bag filled with sweets became symbolic of his bitter guilt. I remember staring at the empty brown paper bag crushed into a ball between my fingers. I let it fall onto my bed and watched it slowly expand like my life in slow motion. Gone was the sweetness it once held; the wrinkled brown paper a representation of my scars.

I'd study his tall presence, his drunken clumsiness, and the tears running down his cheeks as he shook a generous amount of salt on a slice of buttered bread. He stumbled out into the night, shoving the rolled-up piece of bread into the breast pocket of his shirt. I could never figure out why he put food in his pocket.

Shit, school was so damn hard. Did anyone know what our home life was like? When Dad was on a bender he didn't work and became nocturnal. Arriving home at all hours of the night he would wake us out of our sleep to have us sit on his knee as he tearfully asked, "Do you know how much I love you?" We lacked sleep and struggled to get through a school day. It's understandable that only one of us six kids finished high school. I'm so proud of you, Frederick.

Eventually, the electricity and water were shut off because the bills weren't paid, which forced us back to using the pail as a toilet. Mom would lock food away so she could ration our brown paper bag lunches for school. She made our tunics from men's suit material because she couldn't afford store bought and we wore hand-me-down clothes. I distinctly remember my younger brother, Billy, wearing a pair of my yellow, paisley polyester pants. Hopefully he doesn't remember that traumatizing moment. Traumatizing might be a strong word, let's go with character building.

When Mom had us kids fed, bathed and down for the night her day wasn't over. She stayed up for hours knitting our socks, hats, mittens, scarves and sweaters in preparation for the long cold winter. If we were poor, we didn't know any better. To us we had everything we needed.

In the midst of all the chaos, Mom made every effort to try and maintain as much normalcy as possible. Her idea of protecting us was to forbid alcohol or drinking in the house. Drunk men do stupid things like touching young kids, making inappropriate innuendos and swearing profusely. I'm sure Dad was teased by his drinking buddies that his wife had no right to stop *the man of the house* from drinking in his own home. So, every once in a while, testosterone would kick in and he would attempt to bring alcohol into the house. Mom was standing at the kitchen sink looking out the window that overlooked the backyard when she saw Dad staggering up the steps to the back porch. She met him at the door as he entered with a bottle of rum tucked under his arm. Mike O'Reilly, his brother-in-law, was close behind carrying a case of beer. Mom stood only 5'2" but she managed to kick the case of beer out of his hands, knocking him down four steps onto the hard gravel below.

"You're welcome here anytime sober, but not drunk. There'll be no God damn alcohol brought into this house. Not as long as I'm alive!" she yelled as she slammed the door. Needless to say, Mike picked up the case of damaged beer, now dripping wet, and left.

With the sound of the slamming door echoing in her ears she quickly grabbed the crisp brown paper bag tucked under Dad's arm. In a fit of rage, she ripped open the paper bag, grabbed the bottle of rum, frantically twisted the metal cap off and poured the dark poison down the drain. Then, as if taking vengeance out on the rum, she slammed the empty bottle into the stainless-steel sink, sending shattered glass flying across the countertop and kitchen floor. Staggering out into the night he calmly said, with a smirk on his face, "There's more where that came from."

He may have been calm when he left but when he returned, he was in a fit of rage. The loud banging startled us out of a deep, peaceful sleep. My heart was racing with fear as I ran to the source of the commotion. I quickly took a step backward when I saw the 22-caliber hunting rifle in his hands. Standing 6'6" Dad looked like a monster as he tore through the kitchen. I didn't recognize the weeping man who was viciously destroying the kitchen cupboards with the butt of his rifle. He sounded like an injured wild animal.

Broken dishes lay under his feet. In a fit of rage, he dragged the refrigerator into the middle of the living room. He ripped the crystal chandelier from the ceiling and threw it out the big bay window at the front of the house. The refrigerator, tables, chairs, record player all got thrown out as well. The TV exploded as it hit the ground below, laying shattered in pieces on the same soil where his father's smoke-filled body lay years prior, his face illuminated by the flames destroying his home.

I knew enough to know this was his cry for help. He was almost ready for detox.

Unable to control him, Mom yelled to the next door neighbour to call the police, who promptly showed up in two paddy wagons and a police car. Six police officers couldn't calm him down long enough to get him into the vehicle. He was like a savage beast being forced into a cage and he wasn't going down without a fight. About an hour had passed when he gave in to the pleas of my brother, Darren. He was the only person who could calm our dad down and convince him to leave the house. It was my brother who put the handcuffs on our father and helped him into the back seat of the police car.

As an adult it's easy to laugh as neighbours reflected back on and shared stories of my dad's nocturnal behaviour when he was drunk and the measures they took to avoid having him in their home. If they saw Dad staggering up their driveway, they would holler, "Jesus, Art's on da booze close da curtains and shut off da lights!" They would sit in the dark until he stopped knocking, signaling that he had moved on to the next well-lit house. The man never slept when he was on a bender. Once he was seated at your table there was no getting him to leave. Even though he had a Grizzly Adams presence about him, he was nicknamed the gentle giant and was never feared. Drunk or sober they knew him to be a kind, gentle man who adored children and wouldn't harm a flea. But people had families, jobs to go to and responsibilities. They didn't have time to sit and listen to a drunk friend singing, crying and laughing until the early hours of the morning. So, for that reason they hid behind their curtains, where life was normal, and ignored the wandering lost soul knocking on their door.

Dad's diet was a concoction of very little food and 26-40 ounces of straight hard liquor washed down with beer. He refused to accept a meal from anyone stating it was taking food from their children's mouths. Boggles my mind that he worried about what other children had to eat when at times his own had very little.

There was no income when he drank, so bills went unpaid. I remember on one occasion Dad's sister, Edna, and her husband, Ted, were visiting from Montreal. They arrived during a time when we had no electricity. Uncle Ted rigged up a temporary light source by using his vehicle battery. Without electricity the pump to the artesian well didn't work, so once again we had to haul pails of water from a relative's man-made well.

We loved to visit the well because it was home to one huge rainbow trout whose only job was to keep the rock wall free from algae. We loved to feed him by throwing down bugs and worms we found under rocks. Seeing his fish lips skim the surface like a vacuum cleaner made us chuckle as he sucked up the treats. Thinking back and chuckling at the thought, we never questioned where the fish poop went.

Alcoholics Anonymous was not an environment Dad was comfortable in. He said, "I can't do it. I can't sit there and listen to all the sad stories, it's too depressing." With everything Mom had on her plate she realized that if her husband wouldn't seek support, she would seek help for her kids. Once a week she dropped us off at an Alateen meeting where we learned that addiction affects the entire family. We learned that we were not responsible for his drinking, only for our own well-being. Blaming the alcohol gave me permission to love my dad and accept his brokenness.

I've had a hangover before, as I'm sure a lot of people have, but alcoholics drink to avoid them. So Dad would drink for weeks and months on end until alcohol poisoning whispered in his ear, "Quit or die." The detox ritual was always the same. Checking himself into the Waterford Mental Hospital in St. John's was his first attempt to save his own life. Within a day the withdrawal symptoms were so intense that he checked himself out and took a taxi to the nearest liquor store. Within a week he turned to the only person he knew who could save him: his wife.

Cold turkey, in his own home, was the only detox treatment that worked for him and it was obviously the most dangerous. Setting the stage for the ritualistic detox must have been quite entertaining for the neighbours, sort of like the movie *Groundhog Day*. The scene replayed over and over and over with every binge. It took two of us to roll the heavy bags containing all his belongings into the trunk of his car. He would never leave the house in his underwear, so locking his clothes and shoes up was the only way to get him sober. Mom would hide the car keys from us because she knew that, in a moment of weakness, we would give in to the beast that was torturing his body and begging for the key.

Withdrawal symptoms came in phases, each one worse than the last and stretching about ten days. Drenched in alcohol sweat, the severe abdominal pain forced him into a fetal position at the start of the detox. The distinct stench of booze had nowhere to exit but through the pores of his clammy skin. Just writing about it floods my senses with a deathlike odour. I'll never forget it. If I stand next to a complete stranger and pick up that smell, I know that person is an alcoholic.

Nausea, insomnia, anxiety, confusion, fever, agitation and hallucinations followed. The body shakes were so bad he couldn't feed himself. For me to steady his head long enough so he could slurp soup or drink water was an exercise in itself. At night holding a pillow over my ears did not drown out his moans or the sound of the wrought iron bed banging against the wall caused by his violent body shakes. Hallucinations tormented him as he begged us to brush off the spiders and rats we couldn't see. His heart rate increasing, his face distorted by fear, he frantically brushed his hand over areas where he imagined something was crawling. I will never forget the look of panic in his eyes and the sudden jolt of his head as he thought he saw a rat sitting on his pillow. "There's nothing there, right?" he would ask. Every once in a while, you would hear him mutter "Jesus" through clenched teeth as if begging for higher powers to end his misery. When the detox ended it was never discussed.

I don't know who was tortured more through this vicious cycle of invisible abuse, Dad or us. Some days my only escape to try and make sense of it all was to sit at the water's edge of Forest Pond and reflect.

> Dear Pond,
>
> Gazing down at my melancholy reflection in your watery mirror I pondered if there was anything beneath the dark surface staring up at me, me staring down at it. If only the murky, polluted water had a voice, oh what tales you would tell. Would you remember the

number of times Dad staggered around your perimeter, knocking on doors, or the times he drove his car into your cold murky waters while intoxicated? Did you feel any emotion for my brother Darren as Dad dragged him to your water's edge and threw him in, not once but eight times because he was accused of peeing on his friend? Do you wish you could have told the truth, that it was caused by the wind and not intentional? Do you remember me hidden in the trees, sitting on a rock at your water's edge, elbows rested on my knees and my head in my hands staring down at my reflection? Did you taste my salty tears as they fell and rippled slowly farther and farther away into your dark abyss? If only you could talk. What tales you could tell!

Chapter 5

A fish processing plant that reeked of rotten fish on the outside and cold saltwater on the inside was not the place you would expect to meet the love of your life. Especially not while clad in a hairnet, black rubber knee boots and a plastic apron. But I guess there are stranger places.

I was fifteen when my sister and I decided to drop out of the last year of high school to help Mom with finances. We landed jobs at the fish processing plant in the small fishing community of Bay Bulls located approximately thirty-five kilometres outside St. John's. A large yellow school bus would weave in and out of nearby communities to pick up seasonal workers, mostly women, gobbling them up and spitting their tired bones out at the entrance of the plant. The click-clack sound as we slipped our timecards into the punch clock fuelled us to pay day; our reward for standing twelve hours with our hands in ice water packaging cod into five-pound boxes.

Focusing on the fine art of picking bones and worms out of fish, I didn't pay much attention to my surroundings until I got into a good rhythm and was meeting my hourly quota. I glanced up and there he was, peeking at me from around the corner of the cold storage room; his sheepish grin an indication that it was intentional. I really didn't think anything of it because, seriously, a hairnet and rubber boots would not be my outfit of choice if I wanted to make an impression on a young man. Besides, I was fifteen years old. What did I know about flirting?

I found out his name was Joey Williams (no relation). He was a very mature fourteen-year-old with a charming personality that made him stand out like a red Lamborghini. He looked almost Italian with his olive skin, big brown eyes and wavy brown hair as I observed him glancing at me on more than one occasion. At times I didn't know if I caught him looking at me or he caught me looking at him.

I was standing at the order window in the cafeteria requesting a bag of Lays Roast Chicken chips, a slice of Maple Leaf bologna and a Pepsi when I noticed he was standing next to me. Judging from his body language and the smirk on his face I could tell his unexpected arrival was intentional. His nearness sent a sensation throughout my entire body. A combination of intense warmth, head to toe tingling and just pure euphoria. The sexual energy between us was absolutely magnetizing.

He had me at hello and in short order we were spending our lunch and break times sitting in his car overlooking the ocean. Well, it was his dad's car. Joey was only permitted to use it when he was working the night shift. There was no other magical way to end a night shift then curled up in his arms on the bench seat of his car watching the bright yellow sun crest the horizon that separated water from sky. With my head on his shoulder we'd watch the sun's golden rays dancing on the waves of the ocean signally the dawn of a new day.

He consumed my every thought day and night. Like a hero rescuing a damsel in distress, he would gallop into my dreams straddled on Pegasus, a beautiful white winged horse. Like a dance in slow motion, he would scoop me off my feet and twirl me onto the saddle behind him. Resting my flushed cheek on his back, I wrapped my arms around his waist as we rode off into the sunset in search of freedom. We looked like those beautiful sexy models you see on the cover of a raunchy romance novel. My heart was pounding when the alarm clock shocked me back to reality, ruining a perfect dream. Burrowing under the heavy handmade quilts I turned my face toward the sheer clad window to cast a grin at the sun in exchange for warm rays to recharge my hopes. I hoped the dream would return to reveal how the fairy tale ended.

Mine and Joey's childhood experiences were similar in that we both had alcoholic fathers and our mothers were the pillars, the matriarchs, of our families. It was their sacrifices, what they did to survive, and how they protected their children that spoke much louder than words. It's how we became wiser than our years. It's how we instinctively knew that age did not define whether the heart knew what true love was or not. Sometimes it works and sometimes it doesn't. For us it worked, and age had nothing to do with it. Although we were young our life experiences matured us beyond the number that defined our age.

Always a gentleman, Joey was gentle, kind and hardworking. When I was with him, I had a warm fuzzy feeling throughout my entire body. Heck, who am I kidding? I had that feeling morning, noon and night. One day I asked him why he was attracted to me and he said it was how I walked. You see, I inherited the 10-to-2 trait from my dad. If you don't know what that means, look at a clock, 10 a.m. and 2 p.m., that's where my feet were positioned when I walked, turned off like penguin feet. Not pretty, but for some twisted reason he thought it was adorable.

Although Joey wasn't my first love, he was *the* love. I knew he was my soulmate long before he said, "I love you." My entire lifeline was mirrored in his eyes; marriage, a house with a porch, kids, a dog and a white picket fence. We would grow old together, rocking in our chairs on the front porch waiting for the grandkids to come barrelling up the laneway. Without a doubt, I knew in my heart he was that *one* true love.

Rain or shine he would hitchhike forty-eight kilometres round trip every weekend over the summer to visit me. Evenings were always spent outside with cousins and friends, so it wasn't difficult to hide the relationship from my parents. But winter was coming and then what would we do? Expecting Mom to say fifteen years of age was too young to date, I told her anyway and her response shocked me. She said, "Nothing good ever came out of Bay Bulls." I wasn't sure what she meant by that but in my heart I knew she was wrong. Joey set out to prove it. One evening he showed up unannounced at the door.

"What are you doing here?" I fearfully whispered.

"I'm here to meet your parents," he said with a sheepish grin. It was a look that made me weak in the knees.

"Who's at the door?" Mom yelled from the couch.

Based on her comment earlier I was expecting her to throw his ass back out the door. A welcome handshake was the last thing I expected but that's what they did. Dad and Joey stared each other down with a firm handshake that silently laid down the ground rules between them.

"I better not hurt you," Joey later confided with a smirk. "Your dad has a mean handshake."

Earning my parents' respect and trust was important to him. He wasn't shy in expressing how he felt about me around them either. Helping with chores, cutting and storing firewood, retrieving clothes from the line and even doing dishes were the things that won their hearts. There wasn't anything he wouldn't do for them. Over time Mom admitted she made a mistake in judging Joey based on where he lived. To this day she will say, "I loved Joey like a son."

Sketching fairies in a field of tall grass to escape Dad's drinking was replaced with laying in each other's arms staring up at the stars twinkling in the midnight sky. The tall swaying greenery shielded us from judgement as our hot lips met, giving permission to let all inhibitions run wild. Our hands wandered to places we had only dreamt of and before long the soft warm breeze embraced our naked bodies and beads of sweat glistened by the light of the moon. I didn't want this feeling to end, I didn't want to go back to the dysfunctional reality and destruction that alcohol left in its path. But as winter was approaching evenings laying under the stars were replaced with hanging out inside with my siblings.

Our first winter together Joey was permitted to bunk up in my brother's room if bad weather prevented him from hitchhiking back home. We couldn't wait to be alone and would intentionally stay up later than everyone else so we could give in to the sexual urges that consumed our every thought. Our commonsense ability to see things as they are and doing the right thing mysteriously became non-existent in the heat of the moment. Fear of being caught never crossed our minds especially when you consider, on a number of occasions, we would make out laying on the floor in the direct path of the only light source, the TV. Thank God none of the seven other people in the house decided to wander to the kitchen for a drink. If they did it was never mentioned.

When Dad was on a bender, I'd make up any excuse to stay with Joey's family in Bay Bulls, reasoning that it was a five-minute walk from work versus a forty-five-minute bus ride. It wasn't long before I realized that alcohol addiction had different affects on people. Although Joey's dad was a hardworking fisherman and provided for his family, he did love his rum. It was like firewater running through his veins and turned him into a Jekyll and Hyde personality. Over time he became comfortable with me being around and on occasion, when he overdrank, I'd see the other side of him, the side that validated how diverse alcohol-induced personalities can be. Alcoholism is not a "one size fits all" addiction.

A dear neighbour who lived across the road from Clotilda and Joe (Joey's parents), called Joey one Sunday morning to voice his concerns. He said, "Your mom always opens the curtains between 7-8 a.m. but it's noon and they're still closed. I'm concerned that if your dad was drinking, there may have been an argument." It did strike us as odd so we made a few phone calls and learned that, yes, there was a dispute between them. Clotilda gave him some space to cool off and spent the night at her mother's. He called to apologize for his behaviour and after attending church with her mother, Clotilda returned home shortly after lunch.

On New Year's Eve, 1978, Joey's parents were celebrating at a relative's with plans to stay the night. This was an opportunity for us to have our own New Year's Eve celebration. Just me, Joey, his sister, Anne-Marie, and her boyfriend, Gerry. The thoughts of spending the entire night in his arms and waking up to each other was like long drawn-out torturous foreplay. We drank sweet bubbly white wine, ate a lot of food, listened to music and danced until the stroke of midnight. A long passionate kiss welcomed in 1979 and before long we were in bed ripping each other's clothes off. As I get older there are a lot of things I forget but January 1, 1979 is a night I will remember forever. I was only seventeen but the passion and love I felt for this man was unbreakable. Only God had the power to take this man away from me. And then it would be over my dead body.

Everything about that night was magical except when the condom broke—one of those holy shit moments that sucked the air out of the room. We lay there sweaty and panting from the passionate love making, trying to convince ourselves that everything was going to be OK. I mean what are the chances, right? Unfortunately, like a game of Russian roulette, our time was up. Six weeks later, I was a pregnant seventeen-year-old. I wasn't the good Christian girl saving herself for marriage, but I wasn't a tramp either. There were plenty of young girls having premarital sex. The only difference between me and them is that I got caught.

For five months my belly grew like a ticking time bomb. We didn't say anything to anyone until the bump forced me to after five months. I'll never forget the night (not sure where Dad was at the time) when we approached Mom who was sitting at the dining room table.

"Mom, we have something to tell you," I said.

As her pale, drawn, tired face turned in our direction, looking much older than her thirty-nine years, I could see in her empty eyes that this was going to rip the heart right out of her chest. She had never fully recovered from her prior mental breakdowns and I wondered if she could handle our news. There was no easy way to say it.

"I'm pregnant," I blurted out.

"You're getting rid of it," was her immediate response.

I wasn't expecting abortion as the first option. I was carrying our love child. What I wanted to hear was, what's done is done and then we would raise this child with the help and support of our family. I told her abortion wasn't an option and from that moment on, the pregnancy, the tiny innocent life growing inside me, became the elephant in the room. It was never discussed.

Less than two months later Dad, unemployed and unable to provide for his family, moved to Calgary, Alberta, in search of work and a new beginning. Again, he had been sober for over four years. Day by day the dark memories from the past slowly faded into the shadows and with it came a sense of stability and normalcy. The fear of him drinking never completely went away but this was the longest dry spell he'd ever had, so we were feeling more and more confident that he would never turn to the bottle again.

I never questioned Mom about the reasons behind the move to Calgary until I started writing this memoir. Being seventeen and naïve I genuinely thought it was because of the low employment rate in Newfoundland and leaving was the only option. Now, forty years later, when I asked why, she admitted she moved the family to protect me. "You would have been labelled with a badge of shame for as long as you lived in Newfoundland," she said with a sad tone in her voice.

Dad's sister, Leone, had lived in Calgary the majority of her adult life and helped him navigate around what some people referred to as the concrete city. Securing a job and a townhouse rental was all that was needed for the remaining family members to make the move. I remember the excitement of relocating in hopes of a better life but I have no recollection of the details on how we got there. Did we pack up the furniture? How many memories did we purge into the trash? Who paid for the airline tickets? I do remember that Joey and I didn't travel on the same day as everyone else. We remained behind for one month so he could earn enough money to pay for our airfare.

With the family in Calgary I stayed with my Nan who lived on Old Pennywell Road in St. John's, NL. Joey hitchhiked the twenty-seven kilometre return trip every weekend to visit me. There were times his parents let him drive their car, which was a huge risk considering he was underage and uninsured. But I didn't care. I was relieved that he was safe and not hitchhiking. Nan never once let Joey stay overnight. It wasn't proper she said. *I'm already pregnant*, I thought. But back in those days people were concerned about gossiping neighbours spreading rumours. A pregnant, unwed teenager having her boyfriend stay the night would be shocking and the talk of the town. We couldn't wait to start a new life in western Canada, far away from prying eyes and nosey, judgmental neighbours.

We arrived in Calgary to a crowded home, nine of us to be exact. You know what they say, "Love grows best in little houses." Dad secured a job for Joey and my brother, Billy, with the same construction company. The income they earned from back-breaking work in gruelling temperatures put food on the table and a roof over our heads.

Eight months pregnant during a heatwave with no air conditioning was brutal. Mom allowed me and Joey to sleep in the same room but in single beds. Not sure why, as the damage was already done but then again, the pregnancy was never talked about so maybe in her mind it wasn't real. Although Joey worked long hours, he woke whenever I called him in the middle of the night. Most times it was to place ice cold cloths on my swollen feet that felt like they were constantly on fire.

The decision to place our child for adoption is not a discussion I can assign a moment in time to or even how we communicated it to the family, but they knew. We spent many hours alone planning on what we would need, making lists, trying to save every penny, but Joey's income contributed to the living expense of the townhouse Dad rented. If one person lost their job we'd be in dire straights. I wanted to have complete faith in Dad's ability to maintain his sobriety but the question that was always in the forefront of my mind was, "What if he falls off the wagon?" Where would we live with a newborn? We were so scared of raising a child in the same environment we grew up in that we were prepared to do what was in the best interest of our baby. It wasn't an "Aha" moment, more like a "Holy shit, this may be our only recourse" moment. It was torturous.

Knowing this baby had to make an exit soon but ignorant as to how that would happen, I bought a book. Seriously, sex was never discussed so how to have a baby wasn't a casual conversation that popped up over morning coffee. The book was a huge mistake! The more I read, the more I cried, the more petrified I became. I was mortified to learn there were stages of labour, each one more intense than the last, with excruciating contractions less than a minute apart. Reading that the process could take up to eighteen torturous hours or more, that baby coming feet first would be really bad, or I could die, put me in a fit of fearful rage. I threw the book at the wall yelling, "THAT'S FUCKING INHUMANE!" Needless to say, my outburst had Joey a tad scared as well. We were so in love and committed to each other the thought of him leaving never ever crossed my mind but if he was going to, that would have been the moment.

Living in a townhouse complex is similar to living in a small Newfoundland community in that you develop friendships with your neighbours. Kids were playing hopscotch on the road, riding their bikes, skipping rope while the adults (mainly men) hung out in their garages smoking, drinking and making idle conversation. A mother yelling "DINNER TIME" to her kids sent all other children scurrying home and the entire street became a ghost town.

One night, the smell of a home-cooked meal had our bellies growling as we quickly washed our hands. The dining room was small with a wooden table barely big enough to embrace nine mismatched chairs. A plastic eight-ounce Tupperware tumbler was used as a container to hold cutlery and was placed on the table along with the basic condiments, salt, pepper, ketchup and margarine. Mom always made bread by hand even in a heatwave with no air conditioning. Without fail she would present a plate of freshly cut bread at every meal as if it were a trophy. You couldn't help but picture her with that pair of her underwear on her head, bent over a large, flour-filled, ceramic bowl perched on a chair. She always kept enough bread dough aside to make each one of us our own duck-shaped treat, much like a pretzel but shaped like a duck.

By the time everyone scrambled for a seat Mom had our meals promptly served up. Hands scrambled for a slice of homemade bread and then the room slowly went quiet. Glancing at the empty chair, a wave of nausea swept over me. It's been four years. He can't be drinking! He must be helping a neighbour!

Mom sent me to the only neighbour her gut directed her to. The party house. I heard him before I saw him, slurring his words, singing through his tears as he played the guitar. Although I felt sick to my stomach, I didn't show it as I casually walked over to him. Placing my hand on his shoulder to get his attention, I said in a calm tone, "Dad, dinner is ready. It's time to come home." With tears streaming down his face he gently grabbed my hand, pulling me and the extra seventy-five pounds I gained onto his knee. "Please, don't do this," (meaning the adoption) he begged. Those tears represented empty emotions to me. I paused and said with as much empathy and courage as I could muster up, "But Dad, you're the reason I have to."

Until then I had been standing at the fork in the road unclear of what direction to go. In that moment I knew the only choice was the one that would change our lives forever. In our child's best interest it had to be adoption.

In reflecting back on that decision almost forty years later, I still feel the same. No person should have more bad childhood memories than good, but I do. I know for a fact, deep down in my soul, that if my dad hadn't been an alcoholic, I would be writing a very different story.

Not long after that conversation, Dad disappeared. After twenty-four hours we called the police and filed a missing person's report. Within a day or so the police located him at the ferry in North Sydney, Nova Scotia, driving a stolen vehicle. Before abandoning us in Calgary, he bought a truck from a guy at the local bar and hit the road back to Newfoundland with nothing but the clothes on his back. Unbeknownst to him the truck he purchased at the bar was stolen. Lucky for him he was not charged and with the help of family and friends in Newfoundland he made it back home.

I felt partly responsible for Dad abandoning us in Alberta because I told him it was his fault that he would never see his first grandchild. We never talked about it. Dad didn't share his personal feelings much so if it was my fault he left Calgary, I will never know. He took those secrets to his grave.

There we were, abandoned and one month's rent away from being homeless. We wouldn't have ended up on the streets because we had enough family that someone would have taken us in, but the reality was Joey and my brothers didn't make enough money to keep the roof over our heads. Mom decided to send my siblings back to Newfoundland and she would remain at Aunt Leone's with us until the baby was born.

Behind closed doors in the privacy of our bedroom we clung to each other. I lay in Joey's arms as he tried to console me. We were at a loss. Our hands were tied. Where would we go with a newborn? It was a week before our baby was due and we had nothing. It was a lot to expect for anyone to take in a family of three. What support would we have when no one was discussing options with us? I prayed for someone to help us, to tell us not to go ahead with the adoption.

It's not as if we were problem kids. I was a shy teenager and Joey was a responsible, respectable, hardworking young man. Our cross to bear was that we had sex and got pregnant.

It wasn't until this year, forty years after the adoption, that I asked Mom in a phone conversation why no one tried to stop us.

"Oh, they tried," she said.

"What? Who are *they*?" I pleaded with a puzzled look on my face, feeling hurt and betrayed.

"Your Aunt Edna came to Calgary for a vacation when you were nine months pregnant. When she returned to Montreal she called me to say, 'We can't let her go ahead with the adoption. Someone has to help her.'"

The stabbing jolt in my heart took my breath away as I tried to come to grips with what she was saying. Fighting back the anger, tears and disbelief, I said, "But Mom, no one ever said that to my face. Those discussions took place behind my back!"

It took many years and a lot of courage for me to ask Mom that question. I'm not sure if she relayed the facts accurately or if we both realized this conversation wasn't going to make either of us feel better. With that, she changed the subject.

Just a year prior Mom had convinced a very young relative of ours to not give up her child for adoption. She donated hand-me-downs and supported her as much as she could. Why would she not help me? I never asked Mom those hard questions. Maybe because the act of kindness, in helping a single mother, brought her more joy than the shame of having a pregnant teenage daughter.

Shit—writing this tears open the wounds that took years to heal, exposing my heart to the pain all over again. I haven't asked those difficult questions and besides, too much time has passed for the answers to remedy any ills. I now know in my heart that Mom wasn't mentally strong enough to teach me how to be a mom at eighteen. Recovering from three mental breakdowns wasn't easy. Maybe one more would land her in a dark place of no return.

On September 21, 1979, labour began, just like the book said it would. I laboured for twelve hours and, being young and naïve, didn't know about, nor was I offered, an epidural.

There were inhumane sounds coming from the other end of the labour and delivery unit that scared the hell out of me. A woman screamed at the top of her lungs, "Ohhhh sweet Jesus get this fucking kid out of me!" I thought I was going to die! I seriously don't know how my grandmother lived through delivering seventeen babies. After what seemed like an eternity of torturous pain, I finally reached ten centimetres dilated and was moved to the delivery room, which in the 1970s was known as the operating room.

"You're not permitted to see your baby after delivery," the nurse said in a cold unsympathetic tone, as she draped a makeshift curtain across my mid-section. I can't remember if any of the nurses displayed any signs of kindness towards us. But I do remember the cold room, the bright lights, the shadows behind the curtain.

Hours of labour left me with no strength to push but Joey stood behind my shoulders whispering, "You can do this, keep breathing, honey. The baby needs oxygen, you have to push or the baby will die." I didn't want to push. Pushing meant having to say goodbye and I wasn't ready.

The doctor said, "Push, push, push—don't stop, keep pushing."

Joey's hands were behind my shoulders, pushing me forward. With one final exhausting push my baby was born. Laying back on the bed, empty and broken, I struggled to get a glimpse of the tiny shadow from behind the curtain. "It's a girl," the doctor casually confirmed to the nurse in a barely audible tone.

Her first cry shattered my heart into a million pieces.

I covered my face with the crisp, rough hospital blanket and sobbed uncontrollably as my baby's cries echoed off the cold walls of the operating room for what seemed like an eternity.

She howled as they weighed her, checked her vitals and then quickly took her away. A weeping mother with empty arms was all that remained in a room where nurses fell silent. I didn't want them to look at me or touch me. I just wanted to die!

I wanted to hold her but if I did I might not be able to let go. My childhood would then be her childhood. I had to let go.

In the early morning of September 22, 1979, Mom visited me and Joey at the hospital. She didn't stay long because she had a flight to catch back to Newfoundland. The only thing I recall her saying as she entered the hospital room was, "Oh my, oh my!" I translated the sadness in her voice as disappointment. I shut down and don't remember how long she stayed, what our conversation was, or if she kissed me goodbye.

I know I hurt her and she was ashamed, but I didn't have the strength or awareness to fix anyone. My internal struggle dominated my very existence. I despised everything about myself. I was a worthless piece of shit that didn't deserve to breathe the same air as everyone else. At some point I would be discharged. I didn't know what that looked like or if my legs would carry me in the right direction.

Two days later I was discharged. As I gathered my belongings in preparation to leave, I relived the events from the night before.

Standing in the doorway of my room and peeking down the hallway to the nurses' station I could see that it was unattended. I must be crazy! Is it possible that the baby who has been crying for hours is trying to get my attention? It was an eerie, haunting cry and I was convinced more than ever that I was being summoned.

I was eighteen years old and raised to obey and respect my elders. Fearing the repercussions of doing something I was told not to do caused me to hesitate for a brief moment. Regret wasn't an option so, disrespecting authority, I took the first step towards the nursery. What were the chances this was *my* baby crying? I would soon find out.

All the bassinets were lined up in the nursery under a veil of darkness. The newborn infants with bellies full of breast milk looked like little sausages as they slept in neatly aligned rows. One dimly-lit lamp shone down on a nurse holding a baby she couldn't console. I approached the nurse and could barely speak past the lump in my throat. "Is this baby Williams?" I softly enquired. At that moment the baby girl stopped crying as if she recognized her momma's voice. "Yes, it is," she replied unaware of what was about to happen. Grief overtook me as I cupped her tiny little face in my shaking hand. In that brief, precious moment she was mine!

My tears dropped onto her tiny chest as I leaned in, inhaled the newness of her and kissed her soft, fuzzy forehead. Wishing this moment were secretly ours I whispered, "Please remember that I will always love you. Please forgive me."

Panic overtook me because I was somewhere I wasn't supposed to be. For the first time in my life I had defied authority. It was still very uncomfortable to walk so I shuffled out of the nursery as quickly as I could. I didn't make eye contact with the nurse who was holding my baby and she never came to my room to check in on me. She let me have my moment, a moment to capture a mental image that would sustain me for eighteen years, to September 21, 1997, the day I could legally start searching for her.

My heart was so broken that I was convinced I would never feel love again. How could a love so beautiful between two people do this much damage? Love changes, love is emotionally exhausting. It alters your perception of all that is good in the world and slowly, bit by bit, breaks down the delicate fibres of your soul. Love always takes more than it gives, revealing nothing more than empty displays of affection. Children become adults and make decisions that take them down a path lined with life-altering sacrifices. They beg for a reset button, a do over, but there isn't one. I wouldn't trade what I have today for anything, I just wish some of my life lessons weren't so painful.

Chapter 6

Like taking short quick sips of water to get rid of hiccups, I hoped doing the same with my saliva would keep the lump in my throat from choking me. Barely able to breathe and struggling to keep the tears at bay, I didn't make eye contact with the stewardess as she welcomed us aboard our flight back to Newfoundland.

I felt light-headed. Every step took me farther and farther away from that precious little life I had kissed and abandoned the night before in that dimly-lit nursery. Feeling faint at the thought of being 6127 kilometres away from her, I leaned against a seat to steady myself. Although Joey was in front of me, I felt like he was beyond reach. I desperately grabbed onto his shirt for the only piece of security I could find and willed one foot in front of the other until I was in my seat at the window. My yearning to die was much stronger than my will to live. A wave of claustrophobia swept over me as I lowered myself into the tiny seat. The click of my seat belt was like an electric current shocking me back to life, forcing me to breathe.

Blankly staring out the small window past a tiny smudge on the glass I felt a piece of my heart rip and leave my body to float aimlessly outside the bubble we were corralled in. It crossed the tarmac, soared past the treetops and found its way to her.

Noises around me became muffled as people searched for their seats and struggled to squeeze their carry-on baggage into the cramped overhead compartments. The constant clicking of seat belts was like repeated jolts to my heart. I thought I was going to throw up. Then, turning my eyes back to the window, I focused on that tiny smudge, a child's handprint. A tear trickled down my cheek as my shaking hand reached out to touch it, being careful not to erase it.

Oh my God a baby! Somewhere on the plane a baby was crying. My arms may have been empty but my breasts weren't and the unknown child's crying triggered feeding time. Wrapping my arms across my breasts to hide the milk stains on my shirt I desperately begged Joey to go back for her.

"She's crying, hungry, scared and alone. I can't do this," I pleaded. "We can't abandon her."

I loved his big brown eyes but this time they harboured a sadness that offered no beacon of light or hope as he sympathetically whispered, "It's too late, sweetheart. The papers are signed. We can't change our minds."

I felt broken beyond repair as I slowly leaned into the window and quietly sobbed. "Oh, my sweet baby girl, I'm so sorry."

Being back in Newfoundland added to my pain and guilt because I not only left my baby at the Calgary General Hospital, I was now in another province. What if she got sick and needed medical help from her birth parents? How would they find us? What would happen if she wasn't adopted? Would they contact us? If not, where would she go? The questions were never-ending, the answers never came.

Newfoundland was never the same after the pregnancy. The nosey neighbours didn't see me pregnant but they heard rumours. I should have been on the cover of the *National Enquirer* because enquiring minds wanted to know, did she or didn't she have a baby? Was it true she placed her baby for adoption? They probably blamed it on Dad being an alcoholic and Mom struggling to raise six kids under such challenging conditions. It didn't feel like home anymore. I felt like an outcast.

Out of the blue one of Joey's relatives called from Toronto suggesting we move there. They would help us find work and an apartment. Yes, it was kind of them to offer to help us, but it was like adding salt to an open wound. I couldn't wrap my head around their thought process. It literally left me speechless for days. My initial response was, "Where the fuck were they nine months ago? Why didn't anyone offer to help before now? We could have brought her home with us." He knew nothing he could say would ever ease my pain. I was beyond repair. However, I was good at walking away so why would moving to Toronto be any different?

On August 6, 1980, one month before my nineteenth birthday, Joey and I moved to Scarborough, Ontario, on the east side of Toronto. With unemployment rates in Newfoundland at 13.3% and Ontario a meagre 6.9% we knew moving to the mainland would offer us opportunities for a better life. The only thing that brought me comfort was knowing I would be 2889 kilometres closer to my baby.

As promised, Joey's uncle got him a job at Century Concrete Products Ltd. and our one-bedroom apartment was soon furnished with hand-me-downs from in-laws who lived in the same high-rise building. It was exciting to play house, to wake up next to each other every morning and do whatever we wanted without having to answer to anyone. We were finally adults!

We never mentioned the pregnancy and adoption. I didn't initiate the conversation and maybe it was too difficult for anyone else to. It's as if someone hacked out that period of my life with a pair of blunt scissors and discarded it in the trash like yesterday's news. I internalized my feelings and boxed them up to join the skeleton in the closet.

In July of 1981 we travelled back to Newfoundland to attend Joey's sister's wedding. We had started the ball rolling with our own Ontario winter wedding plans scheduled for January 1982. Although we had booked the church and paid deposits on the venue, DJ and photographer, when someone suggested we get married before heading back to Ontario, we did it. Eloping made much more sense especially for two young adults with no money or savings to spend on a big wedding. So we purchased a marriage certificate, bought a white cocktail dress and headed to City Hall. On August 4, 1981, Dorothy Mary Wyatt, the first female mayor of St. John's, married us in the council chambers.

As we sat in her office signing the marriage certificate, Dorothy Wyatt called Mom and Dad in Ontario to give them the news. They were shocked to get a call from the mayor of St. John's but more surprised to learn we had eloped. Years later I was surprised to hear from Mom that Dad was upset he didn't get to walk me down the aisle. Their feelings weren't something I considered because in all honesty I already bore the badge of shame. Why embarrass them more by standing at the church altar, before God, in a virgin white wedding dress in front of people who most likely referred to me as "the one who gave her baby away"?

The flight back to Ontario was an adventure. Someone told us that if we wore our wedding outfits to the airport and said we were just married we would be upgraded to first class.

Thinking we may never get another opportunity we presented ourselves at the check-in counter, me in the white cocktail dress and Joey in his suit. We gushed about just being married and flashed our marriage certificate. When our boarding passes were presented to us we were disappointed to see that we were not seated in first class but with the *commoners*. Oh well, it was well worth the try!

On board, we started searching for our seats and were surprised to find another couple sitting in them. We summoned the stewardess for help. After reviewing our boarding passes she said they made a mistake during check-in. For the inconvenience—you guessed it—we were placed in first class. From the time the plane left the runway until we landed in Toronto three and a half hours later, we were wined and dined in wide, comfy seats at no extra charge. It was a once in-a-lifetime experience.

By the time we returned to our small one-bedroom apartment in Scarborough, everyone knew we had eloped. Saturday, Joey's Uncle George and Aunt Pat invited us to their apartment for drinks to celebrate. They were so much fun to hang out with and felt more like friends than an Aunt and Uncle. Aunt Pat was an amazing cook and was always trying something new. Who wouldn't pass up great food and company?

Usually we do the courtesy knock and then let ourselves in but this time the door was bolted. So, we knocked again and as it slowly opened, we heard "SURPRISE!" All our family and friends, some from as far away as Montreal, were there to celebrate our marriage. It was a memorable night and more perfect than any huge expensive wedding reception.

The memories from our celebration were ones I will never forget but my every day survival was shrouded in a cloak of secrecy with bitter memories too impossible to erase. Not one person who attended our wedding celebration knew that for the past two years every day started and ended with the same gut-wrenching ritual that would last for five years. Upon waking I would slowly roll over to face the window and heave a heavy sigh as I touched my eyes, swollen from crying myself to sleep the night before. The sun was supposed to be warm and bright yellow but I only felt and saw grey. Curling up in a ball under the covers, the loss so excruciatingly painful, I rocked and sobbed until responsibilities willed me to get up. Getting out of bed was like reliving that moment at the hospital when my baby cried to me from the nursery. It took so much effort to face the day knowing I had to put on a brave face and pretend I was over it.

I debated whether to seek counselling, but I knew deep in my heart that nothing anyone could say or do would make me feel better. I was so, so broken and damaged.

Men and women bond with their babies in different ways. For women, the bonding starts in utero. For men, most times it starts when they hold their baby after birth. Joey not seeing our baby put him at a huge disadvantage in trying to understand the depth of my loss and pain. I cried morning and night, sobbing the hardest when he was in the shower where I thought he couldn't hear me, but he did. Early one morning as he was getting ready for work, he couldn't handle listening to my crying and lost his patience. In a split second he straddled me on the bed, slapped me in the face and yelled, "For fuck sakes, just get over it and move on!" Then he left for work, slamming the door so hard behind him that the pictures on the wall rattled. As my trembling hand shielded my stinging cheek, I realized my only support person had just turned the lights out and left me in the dark, alone and more broken.

The two most important men in my life, my father and my husband, had let me down. It was the one and only time Joey had ever raised a hand to me. It doesn't make it OK, but I was so deeply lost in my darkness that I didn't see how helpless he felt. The apology he offered when he returned from work left a bittersweet taste in my mouth. He was genuinely sorry. I just didn't know how to help him help me. From that moment on it was easier to internalize my suffering.

Showering morning and night became my only refuge from judgement. No one heard my cries or felt my pain as my tears mixed with the water, trickled past my breasts, kissed my stretchmarks and spiraled out of control toward the dark, dirty drain where they belonged. My newfound normalcy rolled into days, days into months, months into years.

Two years into our marriage and four years after Juanita's birth we decided to have another child. We quickly learned that getting pregnant would never be an issue for us, as I was expecting within a month. Never in our wildest dreams did we imagine our second child would be born on the exact same day as the older sister she might never meet or know existed. Charlene was born on Friday September 21, 1984, at 1:02 p.m.—five years to the day after Juanita's birth on Friday September 21, 1979 at 1:33 p.m. Seriously? What are the chances they would be born on the same day, same month and only nineteen minutes apart? How much could one heart endure?

My experience with this pregnancy was very different. Ultrasounds, listening to the heartbeat, monthly visits to the doctor were all joyous occasions. I had the option of an epidural, and I was allowed to see my baby, to hold her, to count her little fingers and toes, and to kiss her cute little button nose. Curled up on my chest, her head nuzzled into my neck, I could feel her breath on my skin. Her newborn scent transported me back five years to a dimly lit nursery far, far away. This time was a celebration, this time I was treated with respect, this time I earned the right to be treated like a mom.

For the next six months, I experienced the same terrifying nightmare over and over. In the dream I had fallen asleep with Charlene laying on my chest only to awake a short time later to find her missing. Frantically patting my chest and the bed around me I realized she was gone, nowhere to be found. I would wake with tears streaming down my face, my hands frantically grabbing at the blankets around me. My body trembled as I sat upright on the edge of my bed, not able to summon the strength to stand. Leaning into Charlene's bassinet, I slowly lowered my hand until it rested on her warm belly rising up and down with each soft breath, reassuring me she was OK.

I interpreted the nightmare as a sign that Charlene was going to die because I didn't deserve another baby; I didn't deserve to be a mom. The thought was too painful to bear so I consulted with our family physician who reassured me Charlene wasn't in any danger. Reoccurring nightmares usually stem from trauma, anxiety or stress. The nightmares were telling me I was afraid someone was going to take Charlene, my second child, away from me. Accepting those feelings took some time but eventually the nightmares faded into the dark and never returned.

Crying daily in the shower had eased off because as a new mom I was lucky if I showered every third day. It was Charlene's milestones that sent me to the bathroom, my place of non-judgement. With every "first" I sat on the toilet and had a cry. I'd flush the toilet and, pretending to wash my hands, would splash cold water on my face. Some "firsts" brought more pain than others like hearing Charlene say "Mom, Mom, Mom."

Within a year we knew we didn't want Charlene to be an only child, so we planned for another. Our third pregnancy resulted in a miscarriage. Heartbroken, I blamed myself (as many women do) and accepted it as punishment for having given up a child. Finally, two and a half years later, on March 27, 1987, we were blessed with the arrival of Krystal. Both girls had their dad wrapped around their pinky fingers. Their big brown eyes turned his heart to mush.

I relived all Juanita's milestones vicariously through her sisters. Tasting cereal for the first time, crawling, sitting up, first steps, first words, chickenpox and mumps, teething, starting kindergarten, high school, and dating for the first time. Anything and everything that made me laugh or cry deserved a time out for me on the throne.

Birthdays were the hardest and always started with a ceremonial cry in the shower. Holding a wet cloth to my face to muffle the convulsive weeping, I'd wither down the wall to a sitting position in the tub accepting the pelting water on my back. I'd pray that her special day was filled with loving memories, that she was protected, sheltered and loved. *Please God keep her safe from harm.*

Some days it was so damned hard to crawl out of the shower, but life has a way of giving you a gentle nudge. Not a physical nudge but one deep in your soul that softly whispers, "You got this girl, keep going." Taking a big breath, I'd turn off the tap to close the flow of water that also signaled shutting off my emotions, towel off, get dressed and keep moving.

Chapter 7

Children are innocent, impressionable and more resilient than parents give them credit for. Maybe it's because we don't want to be responsible for messing them up by telling them grown-up stuff at an age when they should be jumping in mud puddles, playing hide-and-go-seek in the backyard or helping to bake chocolate chip cookies.

Just knowing I had a secret that could land Charlene and Krystal in therapy for many years was justification enough to not say anything. I consulted with my family doctor again who gave me good advice. Yes, it is OK to talk about it but only tell them as much as they can comprehend for their age. I remember breathing a huge sigh of relief because giving them a small slice of the truth would be much easier to swallow than the entire pie.

Charlene was six and Krystal was four when we decided to open the Pandora's box. I didn't consider the contents of the Pandora's box to be evil; I was more concerned that the girls might think we were. Vacationing at a relative's cottage in Trenton, Ontario was the ideal getaway, but it took us four days to get up the courage to tell them they had an older sister.

It was a beautiful warm sunny day and after a lazy start we changed out of our PJs and into our swimsuits. Laughing and giggling we ran to the water and played until noon. It was a perfect summer day!

I chuckled as I headed into the cottage to make lunch, thinking that *fresh air sure gives you a ravenous appetite.* Getting the girls out of the water to eat took a little bribery. Telling them I had a secret to tell them piqued their curiosity. I knew I could tell them any secret and they'd be fine but it had to be that one dreaded secret. It was time.

Anxious to get back into the water, they practically inhaled their lunch unaware that I was trying to muster up every ounce of courage I could. We snuggled with them on the couch, took a deep breath and cautiously revealed the secret they so eagerly waited to hear.

"Before you were born Mommy and Daddy had another baby, a little girl named Juanita Clotilda," I softly said. Without hesitation, Charlene asked, "Where is she?"

I explained that we were too young to take care of her when she was born, so she has a new mommy and daddy. Being four, Krystal was way too young to understand the magnitude of the conversation and followed up with, "Can I go outside now?" On the other hand, Charlene wanted to know when Juanita's birthday was. Why would a six-year-old ask such a random question and why did it have to be that question? It was as if she knew.

A few seconds felt like minutes before I could find the right way to say, "You were born on her birthday, sweetheart."

She instantly welled up and a huge drop of sadness rolled down her innocent little cheek. No amount of hugging was going to fix this.

"I want to see her!" Charlene said in a low, soft, quivering voice. "Unfortunately, we have to wait a very long time before we can see her," I replied. "But until then you and Krystal can write to her," I said as I handed her a special journal. "Even if you can't talk to Mommy and Daddy about your feelings write it in the journal and one day you can give it to Juanita."

I don't know what prompted me to purchase a journal or to think it would even help but it proved to be more valuable than I could ever have imagined.

Krystal, so innocent and carefree, ran outside to enjoy the summer sun. Charlene just wanted to snuggle and be sad. What had I done? Was it too early to tell them? Would they be OK?

I was emotionally exhausted at the end of our vacation. Back home, catching up on laundry, I stood at the naked window of the laundry room overlooking the fenced-in backyard of our high-rise building as Joey played with the girls in the swimming pool.

Watching the minutes tick away on the overpriced washers I couldn't help but wonder where the fabric softener goes. Such a random thought! Some washers seem to drink it up before it makes it to the rinse cycle forcing us to use fabric softener sheets in the dryer. Silly thought considering the vacation gave me more important things to ponder. I was an insignificant empty soul floating from washer to dryer observing emotionless bodies moving around like busy bees with one task in mind: laundry. They don't make eye contact, they don't smile, nor do I exist to them. I wonder what burdens besides laundry they carry. Are their burdens as heavy as mine? Heavier?

As the years went by, the girls continued to write in their journals and I invested four years piecing together a handmade Log Cabin quilt for Juanita. Log Cabin quilts are blocks pieced together using strips of fabric around a centre square. One half of the square is made in dark fabrics and the other half in light with the centre square representing the heart of the home. When Charlene and Krystal asked me what I was making I said, "It's a quilt for Juanita so that when we find her, she will know she was loved and never forgotten."

In a way, making the quilt by hand became therapeutic in that I didn't feel as helpless. It had purpose and a piece of me became intertwined in every stitch. When it was done, I placed it in one of those plastic zippered bags that store bought comforters come in and stored it away waiting for the day I would find her.

A large number of family members lived in the same high-rise building on Morningside Avenue in Scarborough. There was no shortage of babysitters as the adults frequently got together on a Saturday night to play cards or board games over a few adult beverages. It was always a lot of fun until Joey consumed hard liquor, usually rum or rye. For some reason it had a different effect on him than beer. It made him angry. His demeanour changed into someone I didn't know. If I spoke to him, he'd pretend he didn't hear me. The first time it happened, I touched his arm thinking he was distracted but nothing, no acknowledgement, no facial reaction. He continued talking to everyone else as if I didn't exist. I'd get odd looks from everyone around the table, shrug my shoulders and continue playing until one night I calmly stood up, looked at him and said, "I don't need to take this bullshit," and left the party.

As usual, the next morning he apologized. Half the time he didn't remember what he did wrong until I reminded him.

Every weekend he would over drink and throw up. When the kids would ask, "Why is Daddy sick again?" I would say he had the flu. Year after year I begged him to choose his family over the booze and for five years nothing changed except my feelings for him. I realized I loved him, but I wasn't in love with him anymore. My childhood, the road well-travelled, flashed before me.

He looked totally shocked when I said our marriage was over. He asked me why and I said, "My fear of becoming my mother far outweighs how much I love you." Mom had three mental breakdowns raising us and committed to staying in the marriage with Dad until the last child left home. I didn't have the strength to make that same sacrifice.

I was so consumed with my emotions from a marital breakdown perspective that I didn't give any thought as to how Charlene and Krystal would be impacted. I wasn't in love with their father anymore, but they still loved him. He was their hero and I will never forgive myself for the pain I caused them as they watched him leave. They were too upset to go to school or play with friends and cried a lot. Working as a home daycare provider for the Catholic Children's Aid Society at the time gave me the opportunity to be home with them. It took a lot of work on mine and Joey's part to develop a friendship without hate, to co-parent with love and respect so our girls would grow into confident women and have healthy relationships of their own.

I truly thought Joey would have fought for his family, but he didn't. He found someone else and moved on. In a way I understood. I mean, we were married fourteen years of the nineteen we were together. We met at age fifteen, surrendered a child at eighteen, married at nineteen and had two more children by the age of twenty-four. As exciting as our first two years together were the remaining teenage years were sad and life-changing. We didn't travel and couldn't afford romantic weekends away. Even though he was heartbroken over the break-up he quickly realized there was an exciting new world to explore. As the months passed, his newfound freedom turned me into a bitter person.

One morning I was watching Oprah interview a lady who was brutally attacked by her ex-husband. Oprah asked her how she was able to forgive him for almost killing her. She said, "Because I decided to become a better person, not a bitter one." Hearing what she went through and how it changed her life was a turning point for me. From that day on I worked on building a healthy friendship with Joey so we could co-parent our daughters together. We became best friends, let a lot of shit go and focused on being the best role models possible for Charlene and Krystal. We became better people because of our journey, not in spite of it.

Joey popped in to visit the girls often and at one point I became concerned they might think we were reconciling. I thought it was important to have that conversation with them. Charlene said, "It's OK, Mommy. I know you and Daddy are happier apart." For me it validated that putting our issues behind us to focus on healthy co-parenting was working.

The girls continued to write notes to their older sister that always started with "Dear sister or Dear Juanita" and ended with "I love you." From time to time I'd sneak a peek just to make sure they were OK. Most notes made me smile but one day I was overwhelmed with sadness. My eyes filled with tears as I stared at the page and read: "Dear Juanita, Mommy and Daddy are getting divorced."

Charlene's sixteenth birthday was fast approaching and sent me in a tailspin of emotions. What had Juanita done for her sixteenth five years prior? I knew it was a long shot, but in 1995 I decided to post an ad in the personal section of the *Toronto Star* newspaper wishing her a happy sixteenth birthday that also included my contact information in case she was searching for me. I waited and prayed as if by some small miracle she would see it. Then it hit me: why would a teenager read the personal ads in the *Toronto Star*? That was just too creepy.

Some days I would imagine that she was adopted by wealthy people, with a lavish coming out party where she would make her grand entrance floating down a winding oak staircase in a shimmering pink Cinderella ball gown. I often wondered if she ever thought about me or even knew of me.

In the blink of an eye it was September 21, 1997, Juanita's eighteenth birthday. My cousin Holly had given me the contact information for Ray Ensminger of Reunion Associates. He was a private investigator from Edmonton, Canada who dedicated his life to reuniting families. The tiny piece of paper had been securely tucked away in my wallet for ten years. Standing in the bathroom I held the weathered, fragile piece of paper in my hand. When was I going to call? What would I say? Maybe he's not in business anymore or this phone number is no longer active. How much would it cost? Could I afford to make the call?

My heart was racing with excitement until I took a long hard look in the mirror. Sadness overtook me as an eighteen-year-old girl stared back at me. I remembered how young I was when Juanita was born. A huge lump formed in my throat as I realized she was too young for me to disrupt her life. What if she doesn't know she's adopted? This could turn her whole world upside down.

My God, after counting down eighteen years I couldn't believe I decided to wait until September 21, 1999—another two years. Twenty years old seemed like a good, mature age for the shit to hit the fan, for me to ruin her life. With a heavy heart I slowly folded the paper containing Ray Ensminger's contact information into a neat little square and safely tucked it back into my wallet.

Standing in the shower with the water pelting down on my naked body, I watched my emotions disappear into the darkness of the dirty drain.

Chapter 8

The morning alarm pulsated through my ears viciously attacking my brain with the force of a jackhammer. Blinded by a vicious migraine, I groped the nightstand in search of the phone to call in a sick day. As I gently placed the pillow over my head to block out noise and light, it felt like I was resting my head on a bed of pulsating needles.

I took a deep breath and moaned as I slowly sat in an upright position. Placing my hand over my left eye, the one to painful to open, I fumbled my way in the dark to the bathroom medicine cabinet. My head felt like it was going to explode. After downing more Advil Migraine medication than recommended on the package, my feet dragged me back to my bed where I burrowed under my fluffy duvet, into the darkness.

When I woke a few hours later the nausea had subsided. The jackhammer in my brain must have malfunctioned because it didn't have the same power over me as it had earlier that morning. Home alone, I slowly made my way downstairs to the bright open concept kitchen to make a pot of coffee. Not the best beverage of choice for a migraine. The comforting aroma quickly wafted in my direction as I grabbed the soft blanket from the chair and curled up in fetal position on the oversized comfy couch.

My eyes hurt with every blink, which is a common migraine symptom that could last for days following an attack. I don't know what came over me, but I stared at my purse lodged against the decorative pillow in the chair directly across from where I lay. I envisioned the tiny piece of paper in my wallet. Time moved in slow motion as I made my way to the chair. I gently sat next to my purse like it was a dear old friend. I stared at her. Reaching inside, I placed my hand on the wallet as if taking her hand in mine. She was the only one who knew how often I'd removed that piece of paper, unfolded it, gazed at the information and safely stored it away. Today was different. Today I instinctively knew it was time.

I don't remember walking to the phone or picking it up. My hand was shaking so badly I could barely read the paper. The information was eleven years old. What were the chances Ray Ensminger was still in business or even alive? I dialed the number. With every unanswered ring my heart slowly picked up pace like a horse advancing from a trot to a gallop, breaking out in a sweat from the effort.

"Reunion Associates, Ray Ensminger speaking, how can I help you?" he nonchalantly recited as he answered the phone.

Oh my God, he's alive, he answered the phone, and he's still in business! I took a deep breath and, trying to remain calm, said, "Hi Ray, my name is Cathy and I need your help to find my daughter." The sigh of relief threatened to unlock the floodgates blocked by the large lump in the back of my throat.

For a brief moment a veil of guilt draped over me. What happened to my plan to wait until she was twenty? She was nineteen years and five months. I figured seven months wasn't going to make much difference at this point. Allowing the veil to slide down my body and vanish at my feet, I stood tall and with the first step taken I was ready to tread the path in my search for forgiveness.

A lengthy version of my story that I had never shared with another living soul flowed from my lips. He was the gatekeeper to my future.

"Are you ready to accept whatever you find?" he asked in a non-judgmental, soothing tone.

"Most definitely," I said, oblivious to the enormity of that statement.

"She might be dead, or abused physically, mentally or sexually. She might be disabled, gay, or in an interracial relationship. She may not want to connect with you. Are you ready to accept whatever you find?" he calmly asked again.

"Ray, I've been counting down the days since I walked away from her in Calgary. I love her; nothing will ever change that."

"Alright then, let's not waste any time," he said.

The gatekeeper allowed me to enter. I never looked back as I shut the heavy gate behind me.

Then my heart sank when he said, "The search could take anywhere from one month to ten years or more depending on how often they moved. Fortunately for you that she was placed for adoption in Alberta because adoption records are not sealed, whereas in Ontario they are. If she *was* placed for adoption in Ontario, getting the information you need could easily take thirteen years or more."

"Starting somewhere is better than not starting at all," I replied.

"I find it helpful to have a letter from the birth mother when I make initial contact with them," he explained. "Can you please write one?"

The overload of endorphins completely eradicated the migraine as I sat down to pen my *why*.

> *February 18, 1999*
>
> *Dear Juanita,*
>
> *I've waited for this day for almost twenty years. Where do I begin and how do I find the words? I do not wish to cause any disruption in your life, so I'll understand if this is too much for you to absorb at this time. Placing you for adoption was not an easy decision to make. Your father and I were very young and both living at home. Both your biological grandfathers were alcoholics and we grew up in dysfunctional homes. We agonized at what we thought would be best for you. We didn't want you to be exposed to the mental, emotional and sometimes physical abuse that plagued our childhoods. I hope we made the right decision.*
>
> *Juanita, you not only grew under my heart, but you grew in my heart and there you will always remain regardless of the outcome of my efforts. I would really like to make contact with you. If you're not ready, then I'll be just a phone call away when you are. If you have no desire to ever contact me, then I feel it is necessary that you at least know your biological*

family's medical history. This could probably be arranged through Mr. Ray Ensminger.

I anxiously await your response and apologize for any disruption this may cause in your life. Just in case I never hear from you, please remember that you were placed for adoption because we loved you. It took every ounce of strength and courage to step aside and allow another's arms to cradle, comfort and love and nurture you into the lady you are today. I deeply regret that we didn't have the support we needed to be those loving arms and guiding hands.

Sincerely yours
Cathy Williams

It was Friday March 5 at 10:30 p.m. I returned home from picking up Charlene at a friend's house and performed the same ritual every day as soon as I crossed the threshold. Before taking my coat and boots off I instantly rushed to the phone in search of a red flashing light indicating a voicemail message was waiting. I picked up the handset of the push-button phone hanging on the wall and followed the prompts to retrieve messages. I was mentally replaying what Ray had said sixteen days prior: "This could take anywhere from a few months to ten years or more." I entered my password, pressed one to hear the new message and heard, "Hi Cathy, this is Ray. I have some great news. I've found your daughter. Call me as soon as you get this message."

"He found her, he found her!" I screamed. I was in tears and shaking all over as I hugged Charlene and Krystal. I immediately called Ray. My heart was racing, I could barely speak when he answered.

"Ray, it's Cathy. Oh my God you found her!" I blurted it out like a giddy high school girl. He started to talk before I could speak another word.

"She lives in Mayerthorpe, Alberta and the reason I found her so fast is because her family didn't move much." I could hear the smile in his voice as he said, "This was an easy one."

By this time, I had lost all control of my emotions. I sobbed through the rest of his conversation. He said her adoptive parents renamed her Kelly. When he initially called her, no one was at home, so he left a voicemail message as follows: "This is Ray calling and I have a message for Kelly. Your friend Cathy is trying to contact you. Please call me back at your earliest convenience."

Kelly didn't have a friend named Cathy nor did she know who Ray was but curiosity got the better of her. She called the number and from that moment on, her life was never the same. Ray reported that she was very excited when she found out who the mysterious Cathy was. She had wanted to search for her biological family but didn't know where to begin or even if she should. Kelly put the search on hold, feeling strongly that her birth mother gave her up so she should be the one to search for her.

Ray told Kelly that her birth parents eventually married and that she has two biological sisters. She started to cry and asked if we were still married to which he replied, "I don't know but I have a letter from Cathy that she wanted me to read to you. Is it OK if I read it?"

"Yes," she replied.

He read, "I've waited for this day for almost twenty years. Where do I begin and how do I find the words?" Ray said she was sobbing so hard that he didn't think she heard the rest of the letter. He suspected she would call back on the weekend and ask for him to reread it to her. I chuckled nervously.

How do you put into words that moment when the needle is finally threaded giving you permission, after nineteen years and five months of brokenness, to sew the fibres of your shredded soul back together? You just can't.

"How do I ever thank you?" I cried. "When can I contact her? How do I go about this? Ray, can you make the arrangements?" I begged.

The process wasn't that simple or fast. Ray had to get her to sign a consent form before he could release any private information to me.

"How long will it take, Ray?" I pleaded.

He said it would depend on Kelly. She can take as long as she needs to think it over and decide if a reunion is what she really wants or needs. I had a moment of panic when Ray said, "It's not uncommon for an adoptee to change their mind and end all communication." This might be all I get or deserve. For now, all I could do was wait.

Ten years prior, I made a fabric-covered album and collected anything I felt would be important in documenting Kelly's roots. I had been referring to her as Juanita since she was born so calling her Kelly felt odd, but I was also comforted that a new name meant new beginnings. I don't know how many times I said her name over and over in my mind, sometimes whispering it out loud to reassure myself that I wasn't dreaming. This was all so overwhelming.

I unpacked the album. Looking down at it resting on my lap I no longer wondered if she would ever see it. With tears welling up in my eyes, and grinning like a silly school girl, I hugged the album to my chest with a happy heart rather than a heavy one.

How could I be so blessed? Charlene and Krystal epitomized the true meaning of unconditional love. They never judged or blamed me for abandoning their sister. Their love never wavered. Now, we were sifting through family photos, laughing and reminiscing as we tried to create a timeline of our family history for Kelly. The girls put thought bubbles with funny captions on some pictures, which brought them to life. They were placed on pretty, carefully-selected scrapbooking paper and adorned with embellishments. Michaels craft store made a fortune off us that weekend. I won't lie, the album was huge, thick and heavy, but oh-so beautiful.

With the girls off to bed, I sat alone with the album. I ran my hand over the pretty fabric cover remembering that night ten years ago when I created it sitting alone at our dining room table while Joey and the girls slept. I held it close to my heart and felt like I was melting with emotions. Picking it up and wrapping my arms around it, I rocked back and forth in hopes it would distract the deep sobs boiling deep down in my gut. I cried till I couldn't cry anymore and then gently placed it back on the table. Content, but emotionally exhausted, I dragged my weary body to bed.

As I snuggled under my fluffy duvet, I turned to face the last quarter moon softly glowing through the drawn sheer curtain. A sinking feeling grew in my gut as my heart struggled to beat. It felt like someone had rammed their hand in my chest and was squeezing my heart. I realized that in order for my daughters to understand the significance of this moment, they would need to live through what I did. I drew great comfort in knowing I would never let that happen.

It's Monday, March 9, a work day. I couldn't concentrate because I was having an internal struggle that tortured me all weekend dealing with feelings I didn't understand. I'm angry because these emotions are interfering with my moment of glory. I just want that feeling to go away. I cried and pondered all weekend. *What is wrong with you, Cathy? You've waited for this moment for over nineteen years. This is your moment. It's not supposed to be like this.*

Why was I so tormented? I should be dancing to a song in my heart and feeling the warmth of the sun in my soul. Depression, a feeling of loss and a heaviness in my heart were lurking in the dark shadows.

I'm hanging onto the memory of a crying baby in the nursery at Calgary General Hospital. I walked away from my child. How could I be anything but a cold-hearted monster? I don't deserve to be happy. If I feel like this, then what have I done to Kelly? What feelings is she dealing with today? Did she know she was adopted? Did she feel she was abandoned, not loved and unwanted? How has she coped? What emotional damage have I caused her?

I pleaded, *My God what have I done?* I had to face my fears head on because running away wasn't an option. I owed it to Kelly. I relinquished all responsibility when I gave her up, so it is now time to take responsibility and let the healing begin.

It was Thursday, March 18, when I received a voicemail message from Ray. "Oh my God, Ray called!" I screamed. The kids came running. His message said that he got a voicemail from Kelly and that she completed the consent form and mailed it to him via Canada Post. He said he should receive it tomorrow, at the latest Monday. Now I was a wreck; I couldn't believe I was this close. Was it possible I might be talking to her the next night? It was going to be one of the longest weekends of my life if I didn't hear from him. With tears in my eyes and a grin on my face I said to Charlene and Krystal, "You know I'm going to be a wreck, right? I hope everyone is aware of that." *God please give me the strength.* How was I ever going to sleep?

After the girls had gone to bed, I sat alone in the quiet living room replaying every moment from the past twenty-eight days. Something compelled me to pick up the note pad and write this poem:

> Here I am
>
> Twenty years ago, I lost me.
> As my lips touched your forehead and the tears burned my eyes. I melted into your soul to always be your guardian angel. If I couldn't have you then I couldn't have me. Somewhere between guilt and mourning I lost me, the happy me. For twenty years I longed to see your face, to hold you close, to look into your eyes and connect with my lost soul. I just realized that in a matter of hours or days the search for me will end and my start with you will begin.
>
> Where have I been?
> *Here I am*

On Friday, March 19, Ray confirmed he received the signed consent form from Kelly. His next words sent me into a tailspin: "Kelly will call you tomorrow."

Tomorrow? Saturday, March 20, of this year 1999? That tomorrow? Holy crap! I turned to the only coping mechanism I had when something was weighing heavy on my heart: housecleaning. There wasn't one inch of that house that wasn't dusted, mopped, vacuumed or re-arranged. Everything I touched was blessed with joy.

The day had arrived, and I was in a panic. What was I going to say? How would I find the words? Thank God it was a Saturday because that would give me Sunday to nurse my swollen-from-crying face before heading back to work Monday. Seriously, I don't know why I hadn't been fired. My concentration level was non-existent.

The only phone in the house was a landline with three cordless handsets. The phone was off limits and God help the person who interfered with the call I'd waited over nineteen years for. We placed the phone in the middle of the living room floor and sat in a circle. Me, Charlene and Krystal just sat and waited. To this day I can't recall what we talked about, what emotions they felt or if we even talked at all. I was oblivious to everything around me.

The first ring startled me. I covered my mouth with my hands as if someone had just jumped out from behind a bush. I picked up on the second ring and managed to nervously squeak out, "Hello?"

"Hi, this isn't Kelly, it's her Mom, Diane," she said in a voice that calmed me. "Kelly is pretty emotional right now and just needs a minute to compose herself. How are you doing?" she asked.

"I'm a mess," I said.

She then said, "Kelly is ready to talk to you now. Are you ready?"

I heard a big sigh on the other end and started to cry before she even spoke. My daughter's first words to me were a nervous, timid, "Hi." Everything I had held in for over nineteen years came flooding out. I had a complete meltdown. Sobbing uncontrollably, I sought answers to the questions that haunted me since the day she was born. My first words to her were, "Oh my God, it's really you. Please tell me you're OK and that I made the right decision?"

"I'm doing great. I'm very happy and have a wonderful family. You made the right decision."

Chapter 9

I felt like that giddy girl, you know the one who got invited to the prom by her high school crush, but she's trying to be all cool, like it's no big deal until she's home alone in her bedroom doing dance moves that should never be seen in public. Visions of hairstyles, nail polish and what to wear keep you awake. When morning comes you know you didn't sleep much but you're so pumped that you jump out of bed and rip open the curtains with such a force it's a wonder the rod doesn't fall on your head, knocking some sense into you.

That's how I felt after my first conversation with Kelly. Except, on this particular morning, when I ripped open the curtains, my right hand hung onto the fabric as if it was a lifeline. Feeling lightheaded I released my grip and as my eyes followed my hand, slowly sliding down the curtain, the room started to spin. Feeling faint I gripped the windowsill and stared down at the heating vent next to my bare feet. I opened the window to breathe in the brisk morning air. I inhaled and exhaled slowly because I heard that's what you're supposed to do to prevent fainting.

Panning the row of cookie-cutter houses backing onto our property, I fixated on the windows with curtains drawn and was taken back to my childhood when Mom would say, "Close da curtains. Ya don't want the neighbours gawkin' in at us." A memory that evoked shame and, for some unknown reason, the instinctive need to hide.

The reflection of white fluffy clouds floating across the window panes infused me with a sense of calm. In a state of disbelief, I buried my face in my hands and wept softly for all the world to see. For the first time in my life I felt free of the chains that shackled me for so many years. I raised my head to the sun, closed my eyes and felt the warmth on my tear-stained face. Today was the beginning of something life changing and wonderful.

I chuckled as I reflected on my conversation with Kelly and her parents the night prior. Her mom said they were thinking of flying to Toronto on the long weekend in May but wanted to know if that was convenient for me. Convenient? Heck I'd cancel a meeting with the Pope if it meant I could see my daughter for the second time in nineteen years.

Two months! In two months, I'd have my arms around her. Unbelievable! Until then we agreed to exchange emails as a means to get to know each other a little better before the reunion. It felt like that first date where at the end of the evening you exchange contact information, but you don't know who should message who first. *Should I give her a day or two? How long should I wait?*

Facing the computer for what seemed like an eternity, I struggled to find the words. This still felt so surreal and much like a dream that would have a surprise bad ending. But there I sat asking myself, "What do I say, how much do I say?" I didn't want to come on too strong or inundate her with a lot of information that might scare her away, so I erred on the side of caution and kept it brief and formal.

> Hi Kelly,
>
> I still can't believe this day is here. Nineteen years have painfully dragged on at a turtle's pace. Finally, all my fears have been put to rest. Knowing you are well, loved and happy has given me an enormous sense of peace. Hearing your voice and talking to you was something I never thought would happen. I haven't slept much since talking to you but oddly feel energized. Thank your mom for offering to send me pictures. I'm sure I'll cry when I see you and who you look like. Right now, at this very moment, I have so much to be thankful for. I can't wait to hear from you again.
>
> Take care,
> Cathy

I hit "Send" and strangely felt like my soul was hanging onto the email like a gift tag blowing in the wind. It was flying through at the speed of light, incased in underground wires, twisting and turning through mountainous terrain until it was presented proudly on her computer like a gift, triggering the "You've Got Mail" notification.

We are two hours ahead of Calgary and realistically she might not see the email for days. This was before iPhones and Apple Watches and any gadget that you could carry with you 24/7 guaranteeing you never missed the notification that read, "You have a new message from Kelly." But I poured myself a cup of tea and sat there, staring at my inbox clicking on the "Send/Receive" icon in hopes of speeding up her response. After my tea, I decided to tidy and dust the living room, where my computer was set up, so as to not be too far away from it. A couple of hours later I convinced myself it was OK to step outside the living room. After all, dinner wasn't going to prepare itself and life had to go on. She wasn't going anywhere, I'd hear from her eventually, right?

> Hi Cathy,
>
> Mom and Dad booked the flight today! We'll be flying in on Thursday the 20th of May. It will be full of new beginnings for all of us. I'm so excited and honestly very nervous. Did you say your whole family is going to be there? Wow this will be quite a weekend! I know we have just begun to get to know each other, and I didn't say much on Saturday, but I am so overwhelmed. It's a good overwhelmed but it takes a lot of getting used to. My parents reassured me constantly that I was given up out of love and that it had to have been a very difficult decision for you. On my birthday they would always say, "I bet there's someone out there thinking about you today." There are so many thoughts running through my mind, mostly good but I do have some concerns. I don't want to hurt anyone's feelings especially my parents. I guess I'm still scared of what's to come. Your openness and obvious happiness make it a lot easier. It's a great feeling to be able to give you the peace that you need. I

> *look forward to May when I finally get to meet everyone, until then take care and I'll talk to you soon!*
>
> *Hugs to everyone,*
> *Kelly*

Before bedtime I asked Charlene and Krystal how they were feeling about what Kelly had said and everything in general. They seemed to be in a good place. Both of them were very excited to finally see a picture of Kelly, to see who she looked like and if their sister had similar characteristic traits as them. Considering they all had the same father what similarities would they have between them? Genetically did they look alike, share the same hair colour and eyes? Was she a procrastinator like Charlene? Did she love shopping the malls like Krystal?

I performed the usual night-time ritual. I tucked them in, gave them a kiss on the cheek and recited, "Night, night, sleep tight, don't let the bed bugs bite." Yes, that was a time before bed bugs became a major nuisance in some cities. Although Charlene and Krystal were fourteen and eleven, I was going to continue that ritual for as long as I could get away with it. It was my way of keeping them little. As I turned off their light and slowly closed their bedroom door I paused with a deep sigh and smiled. "Sweet dreams, baby girls, sweet dreams."

Now it was "me" time. Dishes done, kids to bed and a hot cup of chamomile tea. I wanted to package the gift for Kelly and get it to her as quickly as possible. I placed the album and the girls, journal on the coffee table in front of me. Slowly inhaling the sleep-inducing aroma of the chamomile tea, I curled up in the big comfy chair with the journal, as if it was a copy of the latest best-selling novel. Charlene and Krystal hadn't written much in the first couple of years. After all, they were only six and four when they first found out that they had an older sister. They seemed to contribute as they got older and more frequent after we connected with Kelly.

Their childlike handwriting portrayed their naiveté in what they perceived was a realistic expectation. At their age they thought I would find their big sister and bring her home to live with us forever. Like adopting a pet!

After finishing my tea, I retrieved the quilt from my bedroom closet, slipped it out of the plastic bag and wrapped my arms around it as if giving my best friend a hug. My mind stepped back in time to the cold, dark and damp basement apartment the girls and I lived in after Joey and I divorced. It was a horrible unit located in Brampton. We had to enter through the side door of the landlord's garage. With the stifling summer heat their weekly garbage started to rot and smell within a day. If for some reason they overlooked putting their garbage to the curb it sat there for another week. The smell was nauseating and at times wafted into our apartment.

The extreme dampness attracted earwigs. Earwigs are insects with pincers that lay eggs in damp cracks and crevices. They are harmless but I couldn't convince Krystal of that. When I got home from work the apartment looked like a land mine site with drinking glasses, cups and bowls strategically placed upside down on the carpet. Each one with an earwig trapped underneath. My job was to remove the bugs, because Krystal insisted I not kill them, and then sanitize the dishes she used. Although the conditions were bad it was all I could afford and was better than the alternative, no home!

Every other weekend the girls were with their dad and his girlfriend. I hated being home alone, so I'd spend all day

Saturday and Sunday roaming the malls until closing time. When I returned home, I'd spend the remainder of the night curled up on the couch watching TV until I fell asleep. On more than one occasion I would remove the quilt from the bag, wrap it around me and cry myself to sleep. I'd wake the next morning, lovingly fold the quilt, place it in the protective bag and put it back in its designated corner of the closet.

My beautiful quilt, in shades of green, cream and black floral prints would no longer hide amongst the other blankets in disguise as if it had the same purpose. It wasn't just a quilt. Hours of cutting and piecing squares helped ease my grief. The tedious hand stitching turned out to be more therapeutic and healing than I anticipated. In my darkest moments the finished product wrapped me in hope and gave me strength to face another sunrise. In a few short days it will be in the arms of its intended recipient. Finally, it would go to its forever home, from my arms to Kelly's.

After years of storage the quilt had a musty odour to it so the next day I promptly dropped it off at the dry-cleaners requesting same day service. The clerk informed me that special items, such as wedding dresses and handmade quilts, were sent off-site to be cleaned. I felt kind of honoured that it was placed in the same category as a wedding dress.

My tear-filled eyes looked deep into hers as I rested my hand on the quilt preventing her from taking it away. After what seemed like a long uncomfortable pause, I sensed she understood that this was more than just a quilt when my voice cracked as I pleaded, "Please be careful with this. It's very precious to me. I need it returned safely."

> Dear Cathy,
>
> Diane, Kelly and I will be leaving Edmonton on Thursday the 20th of May at 4:15 p.m., we will arrive in Toronto at about 11:45 p.m. your time. We are looking forward to meeting you face to face, but until then I am sure we will get a lot of use out of the phone and e-mail. I want to reassure you that Kelly has always known that you made the decision to put her up for adoption out of love for her. I also want you to know that Diane and I have thought of you and your pain many times over the last nineteen years. We will always be thankful that we have had the opportunity to love Kelly as she grew from an adorable baby to the wonderful woman she is today. Now that you have found her, she will have twice the love showered on her. I truly hope that you will now be able to put the pain you must have felt for the last nineteen and a half years behind you.
>
> Take care,
> Wayne

I'd counted down 7178.3 days, I could get through fifty-eight more, right? What would I do with myself until the 20th of May? Thank God my work was insanely busy and family activities offered a degree of distraction. Outside of that it was tick-tock, tick-tock, tick-tock.

One night I had a nightmare. I was in Arrivals at the Toronto Pearson Airport, waiting and waiting for Kelly to arrive. Every passenger passed through the double sliding doors except her. She wasn't on the plane. She changed her mind. I never heard from her again. This dream put a dark fear in my heart. Nothing is guaranteed until I see her, hug her and know she is sharing the same air I breathe.

> Hi Kelly,
>
> How are you doing? Your dad sent me the flight itinerary last night. This all still feels like a dream. Are you finding this as emotionally draining as I am? From what I've been told that's normal. I spoke to Joey last night. He can't wait to hear from you and was so emotional last night. He said, "Cathy what do I say to her?" I told him that it might be difficult to think of questions to ask but it will be ok. He asked me all kinds of questions. I told him that I think you will look like Charlene because of the curly hair and brown eyes. He laughed when I relayed that you are a procrastinator as well. I was hoping to send you the album, quilt and other things today, but I won't be able to until tomorrow. The quilt has been stored away for about 10 years and needs a freshening up, so I dropped it off at the cleaners. It won't be ready until later today. I'll send everything tomorrow by overnight courier so you can finally put a face to our names. There will also be a journal from Charlene and Krystal. When we told them at the ages of six and four that they had a sister we gave them a journal so that they could write down their feelings and thoughts if they weren't comfortable talking to us about them. I have read it and must advise you that they

were very young and may have wrote about things that would be realistically impossible to accomplish. So, don't be scared off by some of their comments. At that age they thought that we would find you and bring you home to live with us. I believe communication is so important and we tried to be as open as possible with them. Two weeks ago, we sat and had one of our family meetings and I asked them how they felt about all of this. They are so excited and can't wait to meet you and your family. Now that my head is clear and I can think, I'd like to give you my number at work if you need it and would you be comfortable giving me your number at home? I'll understand if you don't right now. Well, I'm sending this from work, so I better get back to doing what I'm paid to do before I'm called into the Human Resources office.

Lots of Hugs
Cathy

While waiting for a response from Kelly I started recording the names of mine and Joey's parents as well as our siblings. Aside from parents, her immediate biological family consists of three aunts, six uncles and nineteen first cousins. If I dig a little deeper into our parents' side, with Dad being one child of seventeen, Kelly's cousin (first and second) headcount could potentially increase to well over 100.

Dear Cathy,

I can't wait to get your package with the quilt, album and journal. To finally see who I look like and whether Charlene and Krystal look like me. You know Cathy, I can't even begin to imagine what you must have been going through these past years. Mom and Dad often said they wished they could have just sent a letter or a little note to you saying, "Kelly's okay, and healthy." It's ok with me that you want my phone number at home. We do have to start to get to know each other. I'm a shy person and it's not easy for me to open up and express my feelings so maybe emails for now will be easier for me. Let Charlene and Krystal know that I would love to get emails from them as well. Did you ever get that feeling like someone was watching out for you though? Some split second and you say there must have been an angel on my shoulder? I most definitely have and that's got to make you wonder. I'll let you know when the package arrives. Can't wait! Until next time, keep smiling.

Lots of Hugs
Kelly

★ ★ ★

It was Friday the 26th of March, the day Kelly will receive her package, a time capsule of information to help her self-identify with her biological roots. She would no longer question, "Why did she give me away? Did she not love me? Who do I look like?

Who am I? Who are my biological family and would they ever come looking for me?" I would have given anything to hand deliver it her, to be by her side as she connected the missing puzzle pieces. But all I could do was sit and patiently wait for her response to the gift of memories, the gift of answers, the gift of healing. While I waited, I wrote this poem for her.

Does she think of me?

She looks in the mirror and asks, who do I see?
A mirage of questions staring back at me.
My hair, my eyes, the colour of my skin
do I resemble any of my kin?
Does she think of me?

Someone out there must know
answers to these questions I ask as I grow.
My laugh, my smile, my walk
Do I sound like another when I talk?
Does she think of me?

I'm sensitive, loving and caring, it shows.
My personality and mannerisms nobody knows.
From where it all came or with whom do I share
these characteristics, does anyone care?
I wonder, does she ever think of me?

★ ★ ★

She's had her first tooth, walked her first walk,
said her first words, as she learned how to talk.
Another's hand guided her safely across the road,
"Obey all the signs," she was lovingly told.
Does she think of me?

I bet she's learned how to ride her first bike,
Sang her first song on her Fisher Price mic.
Raided the closet, make-up to find
for dressing up was so divine.
Does she think of me?

Her first day of school, was she happy or sad?
Oh my, the friends she must have had.
Childhood diseases, which ones did she catch?
Chickenpox are the worst because of the itch.
Does she think of me?

The years have flown so quickly now.
So many questions, I need answers somehow.
Is she dating, does she drive a car?
Is she out on her own? To get to her, is it far?
But most of all, does she ever think of me?

Your cake this year, twenty candles will hold.
Twenty years of pain, for me, will slowly unfold.
What had seemed impossible is finally here
as I gently touch your cheek so fair.
The answer to my question is plain to see,
I no longer have to ask: Does she think of me?

★ ★ ★

The subject line of the email read "Package Received." I couldn't open the email fast enough. The package she received contained a link to a life she never knew but one she was born into. How wonderful it would have been if her story had a fairy tale ending. The long-lost princess, born into royalty, is found and the velvet-lined package contained a tiara as well as a key to the castle. A closet full of ball gowns and diamond encrusted slippers awaiting her arrival. But, instead, her blood relations are honest, hardworking, medium income, blue-collar workers trying to survive pay cheque to pay cheque and praying the car gets us through another year. I hope she's never disappointed.

> Hi Cathy,
>
> Your package arrived today, and I'm at a loss for words. I was alone and started crying before it was even opened. I skipped the first few pages of the album, the anticipation was killing me and there you were, finally, a face to compare to mine. The questions where I get my height, eyes and hair colour are all slowly being answered. When I saw the picture of Charlene and Krystal, I said out loud, alone in my house, "These are my sisters!" There are some definite resemblances. The quilt is amazing, the amount of work you put into it! You have given me a face to compare to, the pieces to the missing puzzle, and sisters.
>
> I haven't met you yet and I already feel like I am becoming a whole person finally. Your album was unbelievable. Thank you for putting so much time and effort and love into it, I will cherish it forever and I am so proud to show everyone I know. But seriously, seeing you and the girls just made my heart fly. We can't change the past and if you need to hear it from me, then I do forgive you. I sense that you're a kind-hearted, brave and extremely strong woman and I hope you passed even

half those traits genetically on to me and the girls. Last night it suddenly dawned on me. I have two moms that love and care about me. I'm so glad I have you two in my life, and I feel absolutely blessed. I do wish we lived closer together so our families could do everyday things together. It's going to be very difficult to build this relationship long-distance. I wish we lived closer to you guys. I wish that I wasn't a stranger to my sisters, I wish I didn't have to study to remember the names of my aunts and uncles. Our lives are somewhat separate but will always be connected. Can you believe this is happening? The reunion? Oh my God! This is so huge. I just wish I knew what I was, I know I'm happy, but I can't figure out if this is fear or nervousness.

Sending Hugs
Kelly

Chapter 10

Our two-story, four-bedroom house was cleaned from top to bottom and successfully passed the white glove test. Mom taught us that you only get one chance to make a great first impression and it meant everything to me on this, our reunion day, May 20, 1999. Family and friends dropped suitcases, air mattresses, pillows, extra blankets, food and their beverages of choice anywhere and everywhere. Shoes were strewn from one end of the foyer to the other. The house now looked like a cyclone had barrelled through the front door and out the back leaving a trail of debris in its path.

Trying to be the gracious hostess, I welcomed everyone with open arms and a smile but internally I was freaking out. Kelly and her family could not cross that threshold and step into this mess. What are they going to think? What will their impression of me be? The past two months, since my first conversation with Kelly, had left me so emotionally fragile that seeing so much as a crumb fall on the sparkling clean floor sent me on an emotional roller coaster ride.

Slipping away to the solitude of the bathroom I collapsed on the edge of the cold ceramic tub and rested my face in the palms of my sweaty hands. I held back the tears as much as possible because, well, I'm not a pretty crier and today isn't the day to be all puffy-eyed and swollen with a shiny red nose. To ward off the ugly cry I quickly splashed cold water on my face and took in many slow, deep breaths. Peeking over the edge of the towel and into the mirror, I barely recognized the person trying to console me. *The house is not dirty it's just untidy. They'll understand. In the grand scheme of things, who gives a shit, right?*

I realized what I was feeling had absolutely nothing to do with how untidy the house was. For nineteen years and eight months (7178.3 days, 620,205,120 seconds) I internally grieved the loss of my first born; I lived cocooned in my silent mental and emotional struggle to understand the meaning of it all. I emerged changed—in spite of my hardship, not because of it—to somehow see the good in everyone. To be better not bitter. So why, with family and friends supporting me, did I feel the need to be alone? I felt as if I was forced onto a roller coaster ride against my will and trapped in everyone else's emotions of laughter, excitement and fear. I felt…violated.

Nineteen years ago my heart was branded by the cries of an infant echoing through the dark, quiet hallway of the maternity ward. That haunting cry has been my compass to finding her, no one else's. Why now, after all these years of silence, does anyone even care?

My epiphany was in the realization that they care because I opened up. I allowed them to ride the last leg of this journey with me. My past implosion of pain and anger blinded my ability to see that my family were silently hurting as well. I'm not on a journey to understand why no one offered to help two insanely in love teenagers keep their baby. This birth mother, who felt there were no other options, was seeking forgiveness from my family for not inviting them in.

For someone who didn't like attention it became a little overwhelming. "How are you feeling? Can I get you anything? You need to eat something. Would you like a tea to calm your nerves?" *Are you kidding me? Tea? Heck, how about a stiff drink?*

The seconds chiseled away the hours, granting me permission to believe Kelly would soon be within arm's length. I obsessed about time and worried about what could go wrong on the twenty-minute drive between home and the airport. After all, Murphy's Law is "Anything that can go wrong, will go wrong." Amidst the constant reassurances from my family that they won't be late, I chuckled at a comment Kelly made when she realized how many people would be at the airport to greet her, "Wow, I think there will be lips and arms flying at me from all directions." I instantly fell in love with her sense of humour.

Mentally I was preparing myself for what to say when I first met her knowing, in my heart, that tears would inevitably replace the unspoken words. How do I thank her family, who were supporting her on this journey to help her get the answers she silently longed for?

> *Dear Cathy,*
>
> *Somehow it feels like you (and all of us) have known each other for a very long time, like kindred spirits. I'm sure we thought about each other many times over the past nineteen years. I just knew, especially on birthdays, that you would be thinking about her. Somehow, I think we connected on those days, even if it was just spiritually.*
>
> *Kelly is your daughter too and I want you to know that. Yes, in a small way I am acting*

like a typical protective mother, maybe feeling a little threatened. When we brought Kelly home my heart was filled with such happiness and yet there has always been sadness as well because I could sense how very difficult it must have been for you to make such a huge sacrifice. I knew I would be sharing her with you one day. That is what I truly feel we will be doing. I vowed then that I would someday help Kelly find you and support her in that endeavour.

There is a quote by Richard Bach that I have always held dear and it reads "If you love someone, set them free. If they come back, they're yours; if they don't, they never were." Kelly came back to you and I know that she will always come back to me. How can I deny you this time when you gave me so many wonderful moments over the past nineteen years? Kelly truly has been a blessing to me and I know she will be to you as well.

We will all be OK.
Diane

How could this family be so compassionate to my years of loss, pain and suffering? I understood and respected Diane's concerns. Heck, I show up after nineteen years and turn her world upside down. I'd feel threatened as well. We didn't know how this was going to work or if it would work. The one thing we all agreed on was that this was important to Kelly and we wouldn't pull her in any particular direction. She held the reins.

They didn't even know me, but they repeatedly reassured me that we will all be OK. Mother's Day that year happened to fall on my deceased brother's birthday. It was also eleven days before our reunion and the eCard Wayne and Diane sent me was so profound.

> **On Mother's Day, May 9, 1999**
>
> *A small boy looked at a star and began to weep and the star said, "Boy, why are you weeping?" And the boy said, "You are so far away. I will never be able to touch you." And the star answered, "Boy if I were not already in your heart you would not be able to see me." - John Magliola*
>
> Message
>
> Cathy, you have been in our hearts every Mother's Day even though you were far away and we couldn't see you. Soon we will be able to touch you and make it all real. Have a very special Mother's Day. This one is all yours.
>
> Love Diane and Wayne

I couldn't wait any longer and I welcomed the distraction. It was time to slowly get ready and mentally prepare for our long-awaited reunion. My heart was racing as I darted up the stairs to shower. Reaching the top of the winding staircase I yelled down over the walnut bannister, "Can someone hang the welcome sign across the garage door please?" Instantly, "I'm on it," echoed up the stairs. I was never a demanding person or asked much of another but in that moment, I grinned and thought, "Wow, I'm in a position to pull the sympathy card and get whatever I want at the snap of a finger." As sweet as that felt I was too exhausted to take advantage. Although, they did run around like nervous mice when I gave them their marching orders to tidy up and keep the kitchen clean. That was empowering.

I stepped into the shower and as the hot water ran down over my naked trembling body, I buckled over like someone had kicked me in the gut. The urge to cry, throw up and faint hit me all at the same time. The adrenaline was causing my heart to race like I had just run a marathon. Emotions, lack of sleep, and way too much coffee were all contributing factors.

Even though I knew I had plenty of time I rushed through my shower and styled my hair. The skirt and blouse I picked out the night before were pressed and laying on the bed but all I could do was cry as I looked at my clothes. I mean what does one wear to such a life-changing event? Was the skirt too short? I should have known better than to wear an outfit that required pantyhose. What if I got a run in them? Toronto Pearson International Airport was massive; wearing heels would be painful walking from one end to another. Needless to say, I tried on every article of clothing in my closet and finally settled on the original outfit. I tucked a spare pair of pantyhose in my purse and made a mental note to ditch the heels for flats. Scanning myself in the full-length mirror, I raised my hands in the air as a sign of surrender and said, "Well, this is a good as it gets."

With a couple of hours to spare I made my way downstairs and paused for a moment at the patio door to observe the large crowd already gathered on the deck outside. Music was playing, kids were being silly, and adults were chatting and laughing as if it was just another family get-together.

Now there was an interesting observation. I was watching people who hadn't seen each other in a long time interact and reminisce. It didn't matter how long the gap was in between visits they still had memories to share. Ironically, in a couple of hours I'd be back on this same deck with Kelly, her mom, dad and brothers soaking in all the memories they would share with us. I slid open the patio door, stepped onto the deck and smiled because from this day forward, we would be rooted in Kelly's family memories, for all eternity.

Sounding like an annoying kid, I constantly fidgeted and begged, "Is it time to go? Maybe we should leave now?" only to be met with a very patient, "Don't worry, we won't be late." Finally, it was time to leave but I felt people weren't moving fast enough. Our family had this running joke that my sister, Tammy, would be late for her own funeral. She can be late for her own funeral if she wants but today, I'm not waiting around for anyone.

As I slipped my feet into my shoes to start the last leg of my journey, I realized this reunion revolved around much more than just me and Kelly. Does her family ever feel that they will lose her? Her brothers, Bryan and Shayne, now have to share her with two sisters. My God, her mom! She has to be the bravest person I know.

As Charlene, Krystal and I headed for the car I yelled behind me, "Make sure someone locks the front door."

Toronto Pearson International Airport is the largest and busiest airport in Canada. Finding parking and just walking to Arrivals could take thirty minutes. Although it was approximately 11:00 p.m. the parking garage was still fairly busy. We found a parking spot and as quickly as possible, weaved our way through crowds of weary travellers. As I spotted the

Arrivals sign in the distance a family member yelled, "Their plane is early!" I instantly synchronized my pace with my heartbeat and nervously blurted, "Oh my, it's early!"

We patiently watched as people of every age, size, race and colour walked through the sliding doors dragging their overstuffed luggage behind them or pushing carts loaded up with boxes, suitcases and baby strollers. Some people laughed and hugged with joy and others sobbed indicating they were on a journey to say goodbye to a loved one. Some people were alone, which led me to believe they were on a business trip as they pulled the only piece of luggage they had, a carry-on.

Then there was me, patiently waiting for the one thing my heart had pined for for almost twenty years: my first born. My eyes nervously panned the crowd stampeding through the sliding double doors. The longer I waited the sicker I felt. What if she changed her mind? What if she decided she didn't need more? What if this was all I get? Suddenly everything and everyone around me was spinning in a sea of nausea. "I feel faint." Did I say that out loud or just in my head, because no one reacted to the statement? My blouse stuck to my clammy skin as I mentally coached myself, *Breathe or you'll be a sad heap on the well-travelled carpet beneath you.*

At one point I was hugging an emotional Charlene and Krystal, trying to stay upright but be strong for them, not weak. They were so young to be thrown into the middle of my brokenness; it is an experience that has changed them. For that I ask forgiveness.

Then I saw a young man (Bryan) with a video recorder and behind him was his sister, Kelly, clutching her mom's hand. Wayne was behind them with her brother, Shayne. I could barely see her through the tears blurring my vision. She was fanning herself with her hand and taking deep breaths as if to ward off a fainting spell. I held a single pink rose in my right hand and instantly covered my mouth with the left to muffle the gut-wrenching cry welling up deep within the darkest corners of my shattered soul. As I slowly willed one foot in front of the other in her direction, I could see she too held a single pink rose.

Our embrace was met with years of stifled raw emotion. My gut-wrenching cries were followed with the only words that gave me strength, "Oh my God! Oh my God!" When I finally caught my breath I managed to say, "You're so beautiful." I finally stepped back and said, "Let me look at you." We chuckled nervously as I gently touched her arm and then stepped aside. It was time for the sisters to meet and for Joey to hug the daughter he never thought he'd meet.

I embraced Wayne and Diane at the same time. In that precious moment "Thank you, thank you, thank you—" were the only words I had the strength to speak as I sobbed uncontrollably in their arms. It was a hug that mended the damaged fibres of my soul. The journey to get to this day was a long and painful one but God answered my prayers. He placed Kelly in their care knowing they wanted her as much as I hated to abandon her. I have children, I know the sacrifices a parent makes. For them to embrace, love and raise my child as their own is incomprehensible and beyond any measure of thanks. Words will never be enough.

My appreciation was twofold. One was for Kelly's family travelling thousands of miles to bring her to me, to share her with me. The other was for Diane, for being her mom. This child didn't grow in her womb soothed by the beating of her heart and the sound of her voice. She didn't know anything about this child's history, her DNA, her genetic makeup. It was all-in or nothing for Diane. She endured the same sacrifices with my baby as she did her two sons. Kelly is her child and although they didn't bond in utero they did with every new tooth, the sleepless nights of childhood illnesses, fevers, vomiting, diarrhea and the wiping of endless runny noses. Bath time, story time cuddles and goodnight kisses. From toddler to teenager to young adult and everything in between. All the joys and struggles associated with raising a child she lovingly did for Kelly, her child, my child, our child. I'm not dismissing Wayne's role as Kelly's dad—he's an amazing human being—but there's something undeniably special about a mother's love.

Once we got the tears and runny noses under control, Kelly and her family had a quick, albeit overwhelming, introduction to the twenty supporters surrounding us. It was ironic that for nineteen years I felt sadly alone and yet today I was overwhelmed by the support of family and friends. I was appreciative that I wasn't there alone.

Once the round of introductions was complete everyone was instructed to return to our house for a celebration. I was lost in a sea of conversations swirling around me as we slowly made our way through the airport when I witnessed a moment I thought I would never see. Directly in front of me, Kelly, Charlene and Krystal were walking arm in arm as if they had just returned from a girl's night out. Minutes prior they were complete strangers, DNA was the key to identity and immediately they interacted as if they had known each other all their lives.

"They're beautiful, they're my sisters," Kelly gushed as if saying it aloud was proof she wasn't dreaming. "I feel very lucky. I have more family than I could have ever asked for."

It was well after 1:00 a.m. before we arrived back at the house. Even though it was a very long couple of days, adrenaline had us bouncing off the walls. I was surrounded by so much happiness and love. There was laughter amidst joyous tears. We shared stories, ate, drank and hugged often. Our family had an instant connection with Kelly, her mom, dad and brothers.

I took advantage of every opportunity that allowed me to physically connect with Kelly. Touching her arm when I talked to her, brushing her hand as I passed her a drink, jokingly putting my arm around her shoulder as we laughed, or sitting close enough to feel her next to me. She smiled as we made eye contact and there were moments that I wished everyone would leave so we could have some alone time. But I knew the celebration was important for our families to bond.

I can't remember who I said it to but I'm sure I said it often, "Can you believe this? She's here, in my house, sitting on my deck, drinking from my glass and eating my food. How did this happen?" The years that seemed to drag on so painfully slowly were gone in the blink of an eye. Here I am listening to her joyful laughter dance among the air I breathe. It was so surreal; it was so magical.

Diane and Wayne said they often wondered where Kelly's characteristics stemmed from and now it was apparent. "She exudes everything about these people, her warmth, her realism and her personality. Everything about her, we now know where it comes from." It was so heartwarming to hear Wayne say without any trepidation, "Kelly has always been such a great child. Finding her birth family had never been a threat to us. For nineteen years, it's something we've known could happen."

"I feel so happy," said Kelly. "Seeing everyone's reaction and how touched they are by something like this and to think, it's happening to me. It's very wild!"

Tears were rolling down my cheeks as I observed our families interacting. Whenever I cried, I felt the joy of someone's arms around me. Future birthdays and milestones would no longer be celebrated alone, crying in the shower. She was willing to have me in her life and that was more than I could have ever prayed for.

I felt a tingling sensation at the back of my neck that left my hair standing on end. For some unconscious reason I looked through the opened patio door, into the kitchen and instantly made eye contact with Joey. He was alone and leaning against the counter with his muscular arms crossed at his chest. He looked melancholy as if in a state of disbelief, a state of reflection from the inside out. Those big brown eyes I fell in love with over twenty-one years ago filled up with tears as he mouthed the words, "I'm so sorry. I had no idea."

Chapter 11

Another goodbye! The reunion weekend wasn't long enough. In the blink of an eye Kelly and her family returned to Calgary. We continued to exchange emails and phone calls on a regular basis.

Her birthday was four months away and fast approaching. Although it was her twentieth I referred to it as my first. How could I miss my first birthday with her? As a single parent I couldn't afford to fly us to Calgary and going without the girls wasn't an option. However, I could afford one airline ticket. I asked Kelly if she would like to spend her birthday with us. She didn't hesitate to accept the two-week invitation.

The thoughts of having two full weeks with her in our home morning, noon and night was beyond my realm of comprehension. Will she be OK? What does she like to eat and drink? What kind of music does she like? Will we get along? Will she like us? I didn't have a lot of money so wining and dining her in fancy restaurants was not in my budget. I wanted to buy her everything to make up for all those years I missed with her. Will she understand if I can't? I wanted her to see me as a strong, independent woman but deep down inside I hated that I wasn't in a better place financially.

All my fears were unwarranted. She arrived without expectations, bravely accepting whatever world she stepped into. The three sisters instantly hit it off. Their mannerisms were so similar. Their hand gestures, the way they twirled their long hair around their fingers, their body language, even the food they liked. I'll never forget the day she was making a snack. White bread with a spread of mayonnaise. No meat, no cheese, no tomatoes, just mayonnaise. I stopped dead in my tracks.

"What is that?" I asked, grinning.

"My favourite snack," she replied.

"No way," I said with a chuckle. "Mine too."

During her stay with us Kelly would slip outside to enjoy a cigarette and use that time to call family and friends back home. By the end of week one I sensed something was different when she returned from the front step. I thought I heard her sniffling. When I heard her blow her nose, I went to check on her and realized she had been crying.

I said, "Oh sweetie, are you OK? Are you homesick, do you want to go home?"

Her reply was one I didn't expect. She said she had just called her parents to ask if it was OK if she could stay a little longer to get to know us better, provided we were OK with it of course. Provided we were OK? I was ecstatic.

"Are you kidding me, I would love for you to stay longer. How are your parents? Are they OK with it?"

She said her dad was supportive but her mom felt a little threatened. Kelly was so emotionally torn. The last thing she wanted to do was hurt her parents, especially her mom. This was exactly what I feared. Someone was going to get hurt over the reunion. I would never brush anyone's feelings under the rug, especially Diane's. If I were in her shoes, I'd feel exactly the same: upset and insecure about the entire situation.

Within minutes, I snuck away to my bedroom to call and check in with Diane to see if she was OK. Of course, she was worried, mainly that she might lose Kelly to her birth family; heck, I would be too. I wasn't sure anything I could say would ever take that fear away so I offered the one thing that would bring any parent comfort.

"Diane, some kids want to move away from home, explore the big city and spread their wings. What better place for her to be than with family who love her, who will take care of her and keep her safe. I lost her once and I'll damn well make sure you don't."

Epilogue

"In order to heal we must first forgive, and sometimes the person we must forgive, is ourselves" - Mila Bron

So here we are twenty years later. Kelly never moved back to Alberta. She decided to stay in Ontario and has built a beautiful life in Oakville with her wonderful husband, Chris. I proudly watched from the sidelines as they developed their careers, became homeowners and blessed me with two beautiful grandchildren, Avery and Austyn, who call me Nanny Cathy.

I know I'm not the only person to ever say "We take so much for granted in life." I'm so accustomed to Kelly being in my life now that I have to remember to not lose sight of what was, what could have been, and how very different our lives would be had she not signed that consent form back in 1999.

I try to help out where I can, send them on date nights and I buy way too many birthday presents. It's not my fault. I don't buy everything all at once and then I forget what I have until I start wrapping and then it's one of those, "I think I over did it," moments. Christmas is no exception either!

One Saturday morning I offered to take Avery, age five, to her gymnastics class. I thought it would be nice to give Kelly the break so she could focus on other household chores. It was my first time attending gymnastics with Avery and she didn't hesitate to show me where to park, what entrance to go into, where to drop her off and how to get to the observation deck that overlooked the gymnasium. "That's where all the parents sit, Nanny Cathy," she said with innocent authority.

As I settled into my seat in the observation deck with about thirty other parents and grandparents, I couldn't help but feel like I was at an Olympic event. I was amazed at how the facility was sectioned like a grid to accommodate every age group from toddlers to late teens. I scanned the room with such wonderment watching the athletes practice their routines. I was left in awe as I watched children strategically walk the balance beam while others jumped on springboards to propel to a landing position on the other side. There were teenagers, probably as old as I was when I was pregnant, dangling from the wooden trapeze while others swung over and around the parallel bars with great speed and precision. Their coaches supported them through every failed attempt until they landed successfully on two feet. Poised like champions, back arched, shoulders back, chin up, and with both arms raised high signaling (saluting) that their routine was complete. I grew up in a very different world than this.

Suddenly I realized I couldn't see Avery. I slowly panned the crowded gymnasium and became aware that with every passing second my heart rate increased. Panicking, I stood up to get a better view. I tried to look as calm as possible to everyone around me so it wasn't obvious that I may have lost my grandchild. My eyes frantically searched the large facility until I located her. With a huge lump in my throat I breathed a sigh of relief. I don't know why I felt scared. It was one of those "lost child" panic moments.

As quickly as the anxiety subsided, I became surrounded by a soothing, muffled white noise that blocked out all other chatter. As if looking through a telescope, she was all I saw in my circle of vision. Carefree and oblivious to the past events that led her to this day, her tiny petite frame joyfully danced, tumbled and rolled across the colourful play mats laid out before her. Strands of her long, wavy blonde hair had escaped her braid and danced freely across her face. I grinned as I watched her continuously brush the loose locks away from her eyes. She looked so innocent and free-spirited. This was definitely one of my "don't take life for granted" moments. If I had never searched for Kelly, I would be missing precious gifts like this. I wiped the tear that trickled out the corner of my eye. I was smiling for reasons that no else in that observation deck could possibly understand unless they walked the same path as me.

I made my way to the lower level to collect her at end of class. When the door of the gymnasium opened all the kids flowed out like an army of ants running towards food on a picnic blanket, only much noisier.

As I was getting her dressed, I said, "You did a great job today, Avery! I think you've worked up quite an appetite. How about we go to McDonalds for lunch?"

"That's a great idea Nanny Cathy!" she exuberantly replied.

"We better call Mommy so she doesn't think Nanny got lost," I said.

It's a running joke in our family that I have the worst sense of direction!

Would Kelly and I have the relationship we have today if she had returned to Alberta in 1999? Without a doubt it would have taken tremendous effort on both our parts. It doesn't matter where she lives, Alberta will always be her home; that's where her family and her roots are. We are simply an extension of her family.

Initially I thought I was being selfish to want to find her for fear of disrupting her life. The truth is, she was struggling too. She didn't know anything about the image staring back at her in the mirror. She needed to know why she was placed for adoption. Whose blood ran through her veins? Who did she look like? Was there a medical history she should be aware of? All these questions and more could only be answered by reconnecting. Kelly's parents recognized this was a journey she needed to travel. They never pulled her in any one direction but watching this story unfold must have been the most difficult thing they've ever experienced. I can't thank them enough for having faith in a woman they didn't know. They trusted me with their daughter's emotional well-being. They realized we had the same interest at heart: Kelly's happiness.

I stay connected with Kelly's family mainly through social media and updates from her as well. When they visit Kelly arranges a get-together at her house. We eat, drink, laugh and chat about anything and everything. It's these moments that validate how well our families have blended.

2012 was very rough year for me and my family but more so for Kelly. Within nine months she lost her biological grandfather (my dad) on March 21; her adoptive dad, Wayne, on April 19; and her biological dad, Joey, on December 10. She was five months pregnant with her first child when Joey passed away. I truly don't know how she survived that year.

Joey was fifty years old when he lost his two-year battle with liver cancer. I truly believed with all my heart that he was supposed to be my soulmate. We may not have survived as husband and wife, but I truly loved him as my best friend. He was, without any shadow of a doubt, an amazing dad. Maybe the fear of living with an alcoholic had nothing to do with me leaving him. Maybe I was pining for the child my empty arms never held. Maybe it was my sadness that fed his addiction to numb what he couldn't fix. If I could have one more day with him, just one more day, to say, "Please forgive me."

I now have a total of five beautiful grandbabies. Charlene and Ben live in Burlington, Ontario, with their son, Owen, and daughter, Isla. Krystal and Adam live in Stoney Creek, Ontario, with their son, Oliver. I remarried and live in Stoney Creek as well, with my husband, Ralph. Ralph has a daughter, Elizabeth, and a son, Robert. We all live within twenty-five minutes of each other except for Robert, who is in the Navy, stationed in Victoria, British Columbia.

Charlene and Krystal, you have been by my side since the day you were born. You were the only threads that kept me intact, kept me sane. If I didn't have you and the will to find Kelly, I would not be alive today. Our stories are written before we're born. Each day we turn a page until our journey on Earth ends. You were written into my story and although the path has been a little bumpy at times, I would like to think we didn't do too badly. You are beautiful, strong, independent women. I hope you inherited that from me.

I love your husbands as if they were my own sons. I especially love how they love my baby girls. Charlene, when Ben hears a great tune on the radio, he flirtatiously takes your hand in his and dances with you as if no one is watching. He doesn't care that he's a terrible dancer (sorry Ben). When a great song bellows from the speaker there's only one thing to do and that's dance. And now that you have two children the dancing has become a family affair. He loves researching family heirlooms and puts countless hours into creating his own. He has an old soul that lives and breathes the history in all things handmade. I love that about him.

Krystal, Adam almost lost you and his son in childbirth when your heart stopped. When Oliver was safely born, we paced the floor with Adam for about twenty minutes, not knowing if you were dead or alive. He cried, "I can't do this without her." The fact that you are here today reading this is a miracle. While you were recovering in the Intensive Care Unit he stepped up to take care of both of you and functioned on very little sleep. Everything he does for his family stems from the realization that he almost lost it all. He never takes his life with you and Oliver for granted. I am so proud of him.

And those gorgeous grandbabies you both have blessed me with? Well, there aren't enough words to express the depth of joy my heart holds for them. Exploring the world through your babies' eyes is a gift more precious than time itself. I am so very, very proud of both you. Thank you for forgiving me, loving me at my best and more so at my worst.

My dearest sweet Kelly. September 21, 2019 will be forty years since your infant cries willed me to the nursery, the night I kissed you goodbye. I carried that love in my heart until I found you. I loved you then, I love you now, and I will love you always. The similarities between your family and mine are uncanny. Our shared beliefs, morals and values as well as our commitment to unconditional love is the foundation on which our families stand. As long as we have each other we can survive anything.

The relationship you've built with your biological sisters is beautiful to watch. Your kids and theirs growing up as cousins and best friends is a true blessing. Your love for all things Christmas was music to mine and your sisters' ears because we love Christmas too. I particularly admire your tenacity to keep your family traditions alive, like fondue on Christmas Eve and perogies on Christmas Day. Now that you have a young family of your own, you're not wasting any time creating your own Christmas traditions. The annual cookie bake-off with your sisters has now turned into decorating gingerbread houses with five little people, two of which call you "Momma."

From helping you buy a new car, to moving you and Chris into your first home, to crying with your mom at seeing you in the perfect wedding dress, to attending your wedding, to patiently waiting with your mom while you were in labour, to holding your newborn babies and everything else in between are moments I am so eternally grateful for. Life is so insanely busy but I wouldn't have it any other way. To quote my sister-in-law Traci, "It's amazeballs!"

You were conceived from love as much as Charlene and Krystal were. We are all threads hand-stitched together in this crazy patchwork quilt we call life. I am beyond blessed to have you and your babies in mine.

Thank you for allowing me into your life this past twenty years and in the years to come. I am so proud of all your accomplishments. You are brave, you are strong, you are a fighter. Thank you for forgiving me, accepting me and loving me for who I am.

* * *

I gave Kelly, Charlene and Krystal my manuscript to read because I wanted them to be OK with me publishing it. Their blessing was all that mattered to me.

Krystal made an interesting observation though. She said, "Mom, the one person you haven't forgiven is yourself." Her statement caught me so off guard that I was left speechless and struggled to fight back the tears. She's not wrong!

Forgiving someone else is so much easier than forgiving myself for something that has become a part of who I am. When a woman places her baby for adoption it's never an easy decision but the reasons as to why can make it a little easier to forgive oneself and move forward, I guess.

I struggle with knowing I married Kelly's birth father and had two more children. We would have been a complete family unit had someone given us a little direction and support. Don't get me wrong, I'm not washing my hands of ownership. The onus *was* on me to fight for my child. I didn't speak up; I didn't fight for her. I'm angry I didn't know better.

Forgiving myself is not an option. The pain has left a scar that no amount of therapy can repair. For that reason, I linger longer when I gaze at Kelly, Avery and Austyn. A random giggle, belly laugh, or funny comment will have me turning in my footsteps to stare in the direction it came from.

I'm afraid if I forgive, I'll forget and in turn take this life for less than what it is: perfect!

www.ingramcontent.com/pod-product-compliance
Lightning Source LLC
LaVergne TN
LVHW092050060526
838201LV00047B/1323